THE INEVITABLE FUTURE OF WORK

Nuri Demirci López

This book is dedicated to my dear family, to my wife Monique, whose unconditional support and love have been my anchor, and to my children, Alex and Mert, who have always stood by my side, no matter the circumstances. Their presence and belief in me have been my constant source of strength and inspiration.

I also want to dedicate this book to my parents, whose guidance and sacrifices have laid the foundation for my journey. Their unwavering belief in me and their relentless encouragement have shaped my character and fueled my ambitions. To my mother and father, thank you for your endless love, wisdom, and the values you instilled in me. Your legacy of hard work and dedication continues to inspire me every day.

INTRODUCTION

REVOLUTIONIZING THE WORKFORCE : MY PERSONAL AND HISTORICAL PERSPECTIVES

ECONOMIC TRANSFORMATIONS TRIGGERED BY TECHNOLOGICAL ADVANCEMENTS

FROM SCARCITY TO ABUNDANCE

UNDERSTANDING SCARCITY
THE TRANSITION TO ABUNDANCE
DEFINING ABUNDANCE

EXPLORING THE IDEA OF AI TAKING OVER MOST JOBS

HISTORICAL COMPARISON TO ANCIENT SOCIETIES
THE POTENTIAL FOR HUMAN LEISURE AND PERSONAL FULFILLMENT
THE ROLE OF CONTINUOUS LEARNING AND UPSKILLING
THE IMPORTANCE OF FLEXIBLE ECONOMIC POLICIES TO SUPPORT TRANSITIONS
FOSTERING A CULTURE OF INNOVATION AND RESILIENCE
ETHICAL CONSIDERATIONS AND SOCIETAL IMPLICATIONS

NAVIGATING THE NEW GLOBAL ECONOMY: JOBS, JOB MARKETS, AND WORK

INTRODUCTION: THE INTERCONNECTED GLOBAL ECONOMY
EMERGING TECHNOLOGIES AND JOB CREATION
E-COMMERCE AND JOB CREATION
DIGITAL PLATFORMS AND THE GIG ECONOMY
SHIFTS IN GLOBAL ECONOMIC POWER AND EMPLOYMENT
GEOPOLITICAL TRENDS AND LABOR MARKETS
TRANSFORMATION OF GLOBAL SUPPLY CHAINS AND EMPLOYMENT
REMOTE WORK AND THE GLOBAL TALENT POOL
ECONOMIC INEQUALITY AND WORKFORCE POLICIES
PRODUCTIVITY VERSUS INCOME IN THE FUTURE OF WORK

GENERATIONAL VOICES: MILLENNIAL AND GEN Z INFLUENCES ON WORK CULTURE

FROM PERSONS DOING A JOB TO PERSONS WITH SPECIALIZED SKILLS TO DO THE JOB

ADAPTING TO A CHANGING WORK ENVIRONMENT AND WORK STYLE

TRANSITION FROM TRADITIONAL OFFICES TO AI-POWERED, FLEXIBLE WORKSPACES
AI AND AUTOMATION IN WORKFORCE MANAGEMENT
FLEXPRO: THE FUTURE WORKER
DYNAMIC TEAM FORMATION AND COLLABORATION
LEADERSHIP IN THE AGE OF AI AND FLEXIBILITY
SKILLS AS CURRENCY

WHEN COMPANIES SEEK PEOPLE: TRANSFORMING JOB MARKETS

OVERVIEW OF TRADITIONAL JOB MARKETS
SHIFT TO A SKILL-BASED ECONOMY
TRANSFORMATION FROM JOB MARKETS TO SKILL MARKETS
ROLE OF AI IN EVALUATING AND MATCHING SKILLS
IMPACT ON INDIVIDUALS
IMPACT ON COMPANIES
FUTURE OF WORKPLACES
SKILL MARKET DYNAMICS

PORTABLE BENEFITS FOR WORKERS

UNIVERSAL BENEFITS ACCOUNTS
FREELANCER AND GIG WORKER COOPERATIVES
GLOBAL FRAMEWORK FOR PORTABLE BENEFITS
VISIONARY LEGISLATIVE FRAMEWORK FOR BENEFIT PORTABILITY

REDEFINING EDUCATION FOR TOMORROW'S JOB MARKET

EVOLUTION OF EDUCATIONAL MODELS: FROM TRADITIONAL TO FUTURE-FOCUSED
SKILLS FOR THE FUTURE: BEYOND TECHNICAL KNOWLEDGE
NETWORKING AND PERSONAL BRANDING: BUILDING A PROFESSIONAL PRESENCE
COLLABORATIVE LEARNING AND INDUSTRY PARTNERSHIPS

WILL JOBS EXIST IN 2050?

CONCLUSION

REFERENCES

Introduction

The discourse surrounding artificial intelligence (AI) is vast and varied, reflecting its profound impact on modern society and its potential to reshape our future. AI is not merely a technological phenomenon; it is a transformative force that is redefining industries, economies, and the very fabric of how we work and live. Yet, as significant as AI's influence might be, there exists another equally critical domain that warrants our attention—the future of work.

The future of work is a multifaceted subject that encapsulates a range of dynamics including the evolving nature of jobs, the changing landscape of workplace environments, and the shifting skill sets required in a digitally driven economy. It is intertwined with the rise of AI but at the same time different, influenced by other technological advancements, demographic shifts, and global economic trends. As we stand on the brink of what many consider a fourth industrial revolution, driven by cyber-physical systems and further fueled by the pandemic's impact on remote working, the need to understand and adapt to these changes has never been more pressing.

The future of work demands a reevaluation of our educational systems and lifelong learning frameworks to prepare individuals not only to adapt to new technologies but also to thrive in fluctuating job markets. There is a growing recognition that the skills required today will not necessarily suffice tomorrow, and both workers and companies need to commit to continuous learning and re-skilling.

While AI continues to captivate the world's imagination and resources, understanding and shaping the future of work, the future of leadership and the future of humanity remains a paramount challenge. The insights I aim to provide in my ongoing exploration will reflect on these shifts and offer guidance on how individuals, leaders, and organizations can best navigate this evolving environment. This dialogue is crucial, as the decisions made today will lay the groundwork for the workforce of tomorrow.

The essence of this book is to transport you both to the near and far future, providing a lens through which to examine the evolving trends affecting individuals and organizations alike. Every day, the dynamics of work and organizational structures are undergoing transformations, driven by rapid technological advancements and by the changing preferences of new generations entering the workforce.

Technology, particularly digital technology, has been a cornerstone of this transformation. It has democratized access to tools and resources, enabled remote and flexible work arrangements, and fostered new forms of communication and collaboration. From cloud computing to AI and machine learning, technological innovations are continuously reshaping the way tasks are performed and managed within workplaces. These technologies are changing the 'where' and 'how' of work and redefining the 'what' and 'who' aspects of jobs.

Moreover, the infusion of younger generations into the workforce brings with it a shift in workplace expectations and behaviors. Millennials and Gen Z, for instance, are not only tech-savvy but also prioritize meaningful work, sustainability, and a healthy work-life balance more than their predecessors. Their preferences are prompting organizations to rethink their corporate cultures, leadership styles, and even business models. As these younger workers ascend to positions of influence and decision-making, they are expected to accelerate the adoption of innovative work practices, including the integration of sustainability and social responsibility into core business strategies.

These generational shifts are occurring against a backdrop of global economic uncertainty and the lingering effects of the COVID-19 pandemic, which have both highlighted and catalyzed the need for flexibility in the workplace. The traditional nine-to-five workday is becoming increasingly obsolete, replaced by work formats that allow for asynchrony and personalization. This shift is a reaction to external pressures and a proactive adaptation to what is perceived as a more effective and satisfying way to work.

Organizational structures too are evolving. Hierarchical models are giving way to flatter, more agile configurations that promote quicker decision-making and greater autonomy at lower levels. This speeds up organizational responsiveness and enhances employee satisfaction by granting more control over the work process.

The trajectory of work hence is being shaped by a confluence of technological progress and generational change. This book aims to explore these changes comprehensively, providing insights into how organizations can explore this new landscape effectively. It seeks to offer a forward-looking perspective that helps leaders and practitioners anticipate and prepare for the future, ensuring that they are reacting quickly to changes and actively participating in creating a more dynamic and responsive work environment.

Reflecting on my early years, born in 1970 in the quaint town of Waldshut, Germany, it becomes clear how dramatically the concept of work has evolved over the decades. During that era, the structure of work was straightforward and largely unchanged from previous generations. Mornings began early as individuals headed to their workplaces—factories or offices—using their chosen means of transport. The work environment was localized; companies were typically small-scale operations with a predominantly local or regional reach, and the idea of a global workplace was more a notion for science fiction than a business reality.

The absence of advanced technology played a significant role in shaping the workplace dynamics of that time. Without the internet, smartphones, or even widespread computer use, the possibility of remote work as we understand it today was virtually non-existent. People were bound to their physical offices or industrial settings, tethered by the limitations of communication and information technology available.

Fast forward to the present, and the contrast could not be starker. The digital revolution has upended these traditional norms, introducing an era where geographical boundaries are increasingly irrelevant to where and how work is performed. The arrival of the internet and subsequent innovations in communication technology, cloud computing, and mobile devices have dismantled many of the barriers that once dictated rigid work locations and hours.

Today, companies are not only national but often global in their operations and reach. The workforce is more connected than ever, with team members spread across different continents and time zones, collaborating through digital platforms that allow real-time communication and collaboration. The globalization of business has also brought about a diversity of talent, with companies able to source the best skills from virtually anywhere in the world, further enhancing innovation and competitiveness.

Moreover, this technological transformation has ushered in a significant cultural shift within workplaces. The flexibility to work remotely is now a sought-after benefit that aligns with the lifestyle preferences of a modern workforce, promoting a better work-life balance and potentially higher productivity. It has also challenged leaders and managers to develop new skills in virtual team management and remote employee engagement.

Reflecting on the journey from the simple work structures of Waldshut in the 1970s to the complex, interconnected work environments of today offers a vivid illustration of how far we have come. This transformation highlights technological advancement and a fundamental shift in our understanding of what it means to work and how we organize our professional lives. As we look to the future, the pace of change shows no signs of abating, promising even more radical transformations that will continue to redefine the workplace in ways we are just beginning to comprehend.

The landscape of work in the future is poised to undergo significant transformations influenced by a myriad of factors, each interwoven in complex ways. Work preferences, cultural influences, geopolitical shifts, psychological insights, environmental considerations, social dynamics, and technological advancements all play critical roles in shaping how people will work. This book aims to embark on a comprehensive exploration of these factors, delving deep into each one to uncover how they might collectively alter the very essence of work.

As I envision the future, I recognize that individual work preferences are increasingly steering organizational changes.

Flexible hours, remote work, and project-based roles are becoming more prevalent, reflecting a shift toward accommodating diverse lifestyle choices and work-life balance demands. Cultural factors also heavily impact work environments, determining communication styles, leadership hierarchies, and even conflict resolution strategies within global teams.

Geopolitical influences are increasingly prominent, with global trade policies, economic sanctions, and international relations reshaping where and how organizations operate. These changes prompt businesses to navigate a complex web of regulations and cultural norms, influencing everything from supply chain logistics to talent acquisition strategies.

From a psychological perspective, understanding human behavior and mental health is becoming central to organizational effectiveness. Companies are investing in creating environments that promote psychological well-being, recognizing that a healthier workforce is more productive and engaged.

Environmental concerns are also driving change, pushing companies to adopt sustainable practices. While this shift responds to regulatory demands it also aligns with growing consumer and employee expectations for environmental stewardship. The rise of green jobs and industries focused on combating climate change are proof of how environmental factors are becoming intertwined with employment opportunities.

Social changes, such as increasing diversity and inclusion, are transforming workplace dynamics. Organizations are becoming more reflective of the societies they operate in, with diverse teams shown to enhance creativity and problem-solving abilities. Moreover, the growing influence of social media continues to shape employer branding and employee engagement strategies.

Technological advancements are perhaps the most dynamic of all factors, with new tools and technologies continually emerging.

The integration of AI, machine learning, and robotics into the workplace is automating routine tasks, reshaping roles, and requiring new skills. Additionally, the expansion of the Internet of Things (IoT) and the proliferation of connected devices are enabling more integrated and responsive work environments.

In this book, I will explore these factors in detail and also engage in imaginative scenarios to predict how these evolving elements might converge in redefining the future of work. Through this deep dive, I aim to offer a visionary outlook that equips readers with the knowledge and foresight to discover the ever-changing professional landscapes ahead.

Envisioning the world of work as we approach 2040 or 2050, a profound transformation appears imminent. It's conceivable that traditional jobs as we know them might cease to exist, largely supplanted by advanced robotics and AI. This scenario opens up a future where humans are no longer bound by the necessity of labor for survival but are free to pursue passions, interests, and the essence of life itself.

In this future, the role of robots and AI in performing both menial and complex tasks is all-encompassing. Advanced algorithms and autonomous machines could handle everything from agriculture and manufacturing to complex decision-making processes previously managed by executives. This technological omnipresence would ensure efficiency, safety, and scalability across various industries, eliminating human error and optimizing resource allocation.

The shift from human labor to machine labor brings about a critical societal evolution—where humans are liberated to dedicate themselves to pursuits that fulfill their personal aspirations and happiness. This could lead to a renaissance of arts, culture, and science as individuals engage with activities that inspire them, without the constraints of job security or financial necessity. People might spend their time mastering crafts, exploring creative disciplines, or delving into philosophical and scientific inquiries that push the boundaries of human knowledge and experience.

Moreover, this future posits a radical shift in educational systems and lifelong learning paradigms. Education would no longer focus on job training but rather on developing critical thinking, creativity, and personal growth. The emphasis on learning would pivot toward expanding intellectual and emotional capacities, nurturing a populace that is well-rounded, culturally aware, and philosophically grounded.

Social structures would also undergo significant changes. With work no longer being the center of life, communities might strengthen as people have more time to build relationships, engage in communal activities, and support each other's endeavors. This could lead to a more interconnected and supportive society.

However, such a future also raises significant ethical, economic, and social questions. How would wealth be distributed when labor is largely extraneous? What mechanisms would ensure that the benefits of AI and robotics are equitably shared across society? Addressing these challenges would require innovative economic models, perhaps universal basic income or similar concepts, ensuring that everyone can benefit from the wealth generated by machine labor.

As this book delves deeper into such scenarios, it will explore the technological possibilities together with the profound social transformations that such a future entails. By imagining a world where humans are free from the compulsion to work, we can begin to envision new forms of societal organization, relationships, and personal fulfillment, providing a comprehensive blueprint for navigating this promising yet challenging future landscape.

As we traverse the period from today until 2040 or 2050, the concept of work is undoubtedly set to undergo significant evolution. This book aims to chart this evolution, considering the multifaceted influences that will shape the future of work, encompassing socio-economic, geographical, psychological, social, environmental, and political factors. Understanding the trajectory of these changes requires a deep dive into the stages and steps through which work will transform, providing readers with a roadmap to navigate and adapt to this future landscape.

The socio-economic factors will likely include changes in global economic power, shifts in trade policies, and fluctuations in market demands which will dictate where and how businesses operate. For instance, emerging markets might become new hubs for technological innovation, shifting the global economic balance. This shift would require workers and companies to adapt to new market leaders and innovation centers.

Geographical influences will also play a crucial role, as climate change might reshape populations and, consequently, labor markets. Rising sea levels and extreme weather could force mass migrations, prompting significant shifts in where and how work is conducted. Companies may need to gradually decentralize operations or embrace fully remote workforces to manage these changes effectively.

Psychological aspects will focus on understanding the human response to these changes, including stress, job satisfaction, and the mental health impacts of new work environments. As AI and automation assume more workplace roles, the human workforce will need to achieve a new psychological equilibrium, balancing between machine interfaces and human creativity and empathy.

Social changes, too, will be profound. Demographic shifts, such as aging populations in developed nations and younger demographics in developing regions, will influence work participation rates and potentially lead to global talent pools with differing skills and expectations. Moreover, the rise of digital communities and networks might redefine teamwork and collaboration, possibly giving rise to digital-native organizations that exist only in virtual spaces.

Environmental considerations will drive the push toward sustainability, affecting where companies operate and what products they prioritize. This could lead to an increase in green jobs and require existing industries to innovate to reduce their environmental footprints. How businesses respond to environmental challenges will also reflect on their brand and affect their relationship with consumers and employees.

Political aspects will include regulatory changes, labor laws, and international relations, which will shape the operational frameworks within which businesses must operate. As nations grapple with the implications of technological advancements and environmental pressures, regulatory environments will evolve, potentially creating a patchwork of compliance challenges but also opportunities for innovation in governance.

This book will dive deeper into these aspects, providing a clear understanding of each stage of work's evolution. By anticipating these changes, we can equip current and future generations with the insights and tools they need to thrive in a dynamically shifting work landscape. Understanding these stages is about adaptation and also about actively shaping the future of work to foster a more equitable and sustainable world.

One thing I'm quite certain about is that the arrival of the future is not uniform across geographies; it lands sooner in some places than in others. This uneven spread of the future, particularly in terms of work, presents a fascinating area for exploration. My keen interest lies in dissecting how the future of work will evolve differently for blue-collar and white-collar jobs. Understanding these distinctions, how they will unfold over time, and the consequences they will bear on the workforce is crucial.

For blue-collar workers, traditionally defined by manual labor and often seen in manufacturing, construction, and maintenance sectors, the future of work may look drastically different. The ongoing integration of automation, robotics, and advanced manufacturing technologies could potentially redefine these roles. Some jobs might be completely automated, while others will require new skills as the interface between humans and machines becomes more collaborative. The challenge here will be to ensure that these workers are not left behind but are instead retrained and upskilled to meet the demands of a technologically advanced job market.

Conversely, white-collar jobs, typically associated with office environments and roles that involve managerial, administrative, or professional responsibilities, will also experience significant changes. The proliferation of digital technologies, AI, and machine learning will transform these jobs, potentially automating routine tasks and augmenting decision-making processes with advanced analytics. This shift could lead to a greater focus on creative, strategic, and interpersonal skills as critical components of white-collar work. Additionally, the rise of remote work, facilitated by digital platforms, is likely to continue reshaping the landscape of where and how these professionals engage with their work, pushing the boundaries of traditional office settings.

Both sectors will face their unique challenges and opportunities. For blue-collar workers, the key issue will be the transition from manual tasks to more technology-driven roles, requiring robust vocational training and education systems. For white-collar professionals, the challenge will be to continually adapt to rapidly changing technologies and maintain relevance in an increasingly automated world.

Moreover, as we consider how these job categories are evolving, it's imperative to also examine how both sets of workers will address the broader economic needs. As the economy transforms through technology and globalization, corporations and workers alike must adapt. Companies will need to invest in training and development while also innovating in how they manage and support their workforce. They will need to find a balance between leveraging technology for efficiency and maintaining a workforce that is motivated, skilled, and capable of performing in a changing landscape.

Looking ahead, it is evident that the future of work will be marked by disparities in how quickly and profoundly different types of work are transformed. These differences will require a thorough examination and understanding of specific sectors and job types. As this book progresses, we will deep dive into each category—blue-collar and white-collar—to unravel how technological advancements and other factors discussed in the introduction are reshaping their professional lives. This exploration will highlight the emerging trends and offer insights into preparing for and thriving in the future work environment that awaits us.

The relentless pace of technological and social change continues to make the future of work an endlessly fascinating subject for speculation and study. Imagining the kinds of jobs that might emerge by 2040 is particularly intriguing. Consider the landscape twenty years ago, when concepts like Instagram, YouTube, and AI prompt engineers were not just unforeseen but seemingly implausible. These platforms and roles have since emerged and have created ecosystems of employment and innovation around them, demonstrating the transformative impact of digital and social media on global work dynamics.

As we look to the future, the emergence of new job roles is inevitable, driven by advancements in technology, shifts in consumer behavior, and changes in the global economy. For instance, the expansion of virtual and augmented reality technologies might give rise to Virtual Reality Experience

Designers and Augmented Reality Product Developers, professionals dedicated to creating immersive digital environments for education, entertainment, and business. Similarly, as our reliance on AI grows, we might see roles like AI Ethics Compliance Officers, ensuring that AI systems are designed and deployed responsibly.

The burgeoning field of biotechnology could lead to roles such as Genetic Modification Specialists or Bio-Privacy Managers, addressing the ethical, legal, and social implications of gene editing and biometrics. Meanwhile, the intensifying need to address climate change might spur positions like Carbon Capture Technicians and Urban Farming Consultants, focused on sustainability and food security in increasingly urbanized landscapes.

Furthermore, as space exploration advances, we could anticipate roles such as Off-Planet Habitat Architects or Asteroid Mining Engineers, which sound like science fiction but could soon be reality. The commercialization of space travel and the potential colonization of other planets would require a host of new professions, from Space Tourism Guides to Interplanetary Communication Specialists.

In addition to technological drivers, social and cultural shifts will also play a significant role in the creation of new job types. For example, as global connectivity increases and cultural barriers decrease, we might see a rise in Global System Navigators, professionals who help individuals and businesses navigate the complexities of a connected world, from legal and financial compliance across borders to cultural brokerage.

Imagining these future roles requires a blend of creativity, insight into current trends, and an understanding of the forces shaping our world. It's about anticipating needs and possibilities that don't yet exist but could become crucial in the near future. In exploring these potential new professions, this book will delve into the technologies, societal shifts, and economic changes driving the evolution of work, providing a visionary glimpse into the myriad ways people might earn a living in the decades to come. As we explore these possibilities, the aim is not only to predict but to inspire preparation and adaptation, ensuring that as these new roles emerge, individuals and societies at large are ready to embrace and excel in them.

It is indeed captivating to envision how the nature of work will evolve, and also how a typical day for a future worker might unfold. The scenarios often depicted in science fiction—where technology seamlessly integrates into our daily routines, making life more convenient and tailored to individual preferences—may not be far from becoming a reality. Picture a morning where, as you enjoy your coffee, job opportunities tailored to your specific skills and preferences find their way to you, without the need for traditional job applications.

Imagine a world where the job market operates much like the stock market does today. In this futuristic marketplace, individuals' skills and competencies are traded like stocks. Just as investors speculate on the value of shares based on company performance predictions, in the future, companies and other entities might invest in people's skills based on projected demand and potential. This could radically transform the concept of employment and career development. Your skill sets, perhaps constantly updated and validated through continuous learning and micro-credentialing systems, could fluctuate in value based on market needs, technological advancements, or economic shifts.

In such a world, freelancers might dominate the workforce, engaging in projects and tasks dynamically matched to their evolving skill sets by sophisticated AI-driven platforms. These platforms could analyze data from various sources to predict which skills are likely to be in demand and guide workers toward future learning paths and opportunities. Workers might receive notifications of job matches directly, and with blockchain technology, they could instantly enter into secure, transparent contracts without the need for intermediaries.

Moreover, highly interpersonal skills, often undervalued in traditional settings, could gain substantial market value. Skills such as empathy, collaboration, and Emotional Intelligence (EQ) might be assessed and quantified, perhaps through advanced biometric and AI systems that provide a more nuanced understanding of human interactions and their impacts on productivity and work environment quality.

This system could also lead to a more meritocratic job market where biases in hiring are significantly reduced. Algorithms designed to be fair and unbiased could level the playing field, offering job opportunities based solely on the match between a company's needs and a worker's skills and potential contributions, rather than on background, gender, location or race.

However, such a radical transformation would not be without its challenges and ethical considerations. The idea of skills being traded on a market raises questions about privacy, the commodification of personal attributes, and the potential for new forms of inequality. It would be crucial to establish robust regulatory frameworks to ensure that while the market for skills is efficient, it is also fair and humane.

As we cover these fascinating possibilities, this book will explore both the immense opportunities and the significant challenges of this potential future. We will examine how such a day-to-day experience would affect workers' lifestyles, societal norms, and even global economic structures. By probing these futuristic scenarios, the goal is to offer a deeper understanding of the possibilities ahead, encouraging readers to think critically about the implications and prepare for an increasingly unpredictable world of work.

Revolutionizing the Workforce : My Personal and Historical Perspectives

In the summer of 1952, as the world slowly recovered from the Second World War, the global economy and job markets were beginning to show signs of revitalization. It was during this time of cautious optimism that my father, then a spirited 18-year-old, discovered a life-changing opportunity nestled within the pages of a local newspaper—a rare find in his small village.

The job advertisement, calling for workers at a Swiss factory, seemed almost unbelievable to the villagers, for whom international travel was a luxury beyond reach. In that era, local newspapers primarily served small community interests and rarely featured opportunities beyond regional boundaries. This particular posting was a window to a broader world, promising new possibilities that were previously unimaginable to a young man from a modest background.

With no access to typewriters or modern conveniences, my father crafted his application by hand. Each word was carefully penned, reflecting both his determination and the meticulous nature required by the task. After submitting his simple paper resume—a stark contrast to the digital applications of today—he started a journey fueled by hope and the supportive murmurs of his community.

Months of waiting followed, during which the local agency became a daily pilgrimage site for my father. He wasn't alone; other hopefuls from his village also gathered there, each eager for news that might lift them from the familiarity of their daily routines to the promise of stable employment and new experiences abroad.

The economic landscape of the early 1950s was marked by a burgeoning shift toward rebuilding industries and expanding international trade, setting the stage for what would later be known as the post-war economic boom. Factories across Europe were ramping up production to meet the increasing consumer demand, and countries like Switzerland were on the lookout for labor to power their industrial engines.

When the long-awaited response finally arrived, it brought with it a job offer and, together with it, a confirmation that the world was knitting itself back together, redefining boundaries, and creating opportunities for even those in the most remote parts of the world. My father's acceptance into the factory was more than just employment for him, it was the step forward toward a new beginning that symbolized the resilience and adaptability that identified his generation.

Upon his arrival in Switzerland one cold and rainy evening, along with several fellow villagers, my father was filled with a mix of apprehension and excitement. The factory that had contracted them sent a van to pick them up—a gesture that marked the beginning of a new chapter in their lives. As they drove through the unfamiliar streets toward their future shared home, the reality of their new jobs and lives in a foreign land began to sink in.

My father, a sturdy man of medium height but remarkable strength and agility, found himself in a sprawling textile factory. He was assigned to operate a somewhat primitive machine—one that, despite the march of technology, still required careful human control. Unlike the fully automated behemoths of modern factories, this machine needed a skilled operator, a role my father took pride in.

In those years, the world economy was undergoing a massive transformation. The post-war era had ignited a boom in industrial production and international trade, fueled by reconstruction efforts and the expansion of global markets. Switzerland, known for its precision engineering and high-quality manufacturing, was at the forefront of this industrial surge. Textile manufacturing, in particular, saw significant advancements with the introduction of synthetic fibers and automated weaving technologies, which increased production rates and reduced costs.

Amidst this economic upswing, my father thrived. He embraced the challenges of his new environment, learning German, earning a respectable income, and forming friendships that bridged cultural divides. However, the shadow of technological advancement loomed large. As more sophisticated machines began to replace the older models, anxiety spread among the workforce. Many of his colleagues feared redundancy as the factory leaned toward more automated processes.

Meetings between the workers, management, and labor syndicates became frequent, as discussions about job security and the future of work dominated conversations. Despite the uncertainty, my father's resilience and adaptability shone through. Recognizing the inevitability of technological progression, he chose to engage directly with the new machines rather than shy away from them. He spent extra hours at the factory, often staying late into the night, learning the intricacies of the advanced equipment.

This proactive approach did not go unnoticed. Within months, his efforts to master the new technology paid off. He was promoted to one of the core operators of the sophisticated machinery, a role that secured his position and marked him as an important member of the factory's workforce.

This period of my father's life exemplifies a broader story that was unfolding across industrialized nations. While automation brought about efficiency and economic growth, it also required workers to adapt to the changing landscape of employment, in addition to how and where the work was done.

The Industrial Revolution continued its evolution post-1952. The use of non-AI machines to simplify repetitive tasks was becoming increasingly common in factories across Europe, signaling a shift toward more efficient production methods.

The textile factory where my father worked was no exception. It began integrating more complex machinery designed to streamline the manufacturing process, focusing on increasing output while reducing the physical strain on workers. These machines, though not governed by AI, were sophisticated for their time, embodying the era's cutting-edge mechanical technology. They were designed to perform repetitive tasks with precision and consistency, which previously would have required the laborious effort of several workers, hence changing the type of work and effort workers needed to apply in their day-to-day.

My father, who had already demonstrated his adaptability and willingness to learn, found himself at the forefront of this shift. The new machines were complex and required a detailed understanding of mechanical operations to run effectively. Remembering his earlier commitment to learning the intricacies of the earlier machines, he applied the same diligence and curiosity to these advanced systems. He remembers he was literally working day and night.

This period marked a significant evolution in the factory's operation. The introduction of these machines altered the production process, and it reshaped the skills landscape within the workforce. Workers who, like my father, were willing to adapt and upskill, found new opportunities for advancement. All of a sudden training centers and books on how those machines operated started to pop up.

However, for those resistant to change or unwilling to learn, the transition posed a threat to their continued employment.

In this transformative environment, my father continued to thrive. His days were spent managing the delicate balance between machine efficiency and product quality, ensuring that the mechanized processes did not compromise the textiles' integrity. Nights were often dedicated to studying the mechanics of the new equipment, understanding each gear and lever's role in the larger system. His efforts paid off, and he soon became known as a machine specialist within the factory. His efforts really paid off. He was not the "farmer boy" of his village anymore, he was a machine specialist.

This era of mechanization extended beyond the textile industry, reflecting a broader trend across various sectors. Factories worldwide were adopting similar technologies, each aiming to capitalize on the potential for increased productivity and reduced labor costs. This shift was part of the broader story of the mid-20th-century economic boom, fueled by technological advancements and the globalization of production networks.

As these changes unfolded, the global economy witnessed substantial growth, with industries like automotive, aerospace, and electronics also embracing mechanization. This period of industrial and economic expansion laid the groundwork for future innovations in automation and technology.

Through the lens of my father's experience, I can clearly see the dual nature of technological progress. It brought about significant economic growth and opportunities for those willing to adapt, yet it also required a rethinking of traditional labor roles and practices. His story exemplifies the journey of many workers of his generation—navigating the challenges of new technologies while seizing the opportunities they presented. As we move forward in this story, we'll see how these foundational changes set the stage for the next technological leap forward, preparing the workforce for the advent of digital technology and, eventually, AI.

As the 1950s marched onward, the world my father knew began to transform in profound ways. The machines that had once seemed formidable now hummed rhythmically in the background of his daily work life in the Swiss textile factory. Yet, the changes weren't confined within factory walls; they rippled out, reshaping economies and societies at large.

As industrial growth surged, a parallel shift was taking place—a movement from the fields and factories into burgeoning office spaces. This shift was not just physical but cultural, reflecting a world that was rapidly expanding beyond local markets to a more interconnected global economy.

For my father, the impact of these changes became evident when the factory management introduced a small administrative unit. It was a modest beginning, with just a few desks and typewriters, yet it represented the dawn of a new era in work. My father watched as some of his colleagues transitioned from the factory floor to these new roles. They swapped their mechanical tools for pens and papers, their workbenches for desks. This shift marked a significant change in the concept of work—from physical labor to one that required new skills like typing and basic accounting.

This burgeoning office culture was a microcosm of a larger shift across Europe and North America, where the service sector began to expand dramatically. Offices were becoming the new centers of work, driving demand for white-collar workers. These workers engaged not in the production of physical goods but also in the management, administration, and sale of those goods.

My father saw the writing on the wall. With machines taking over more of the manual labor in the factory, he knew that securing his future meant adapting to this new world. Driven by a desire to secure a stable position, he began to take night classes offered by the factory, learning the basics of administration and German business correspondence.

This adaptation was not without its challenges. The office environment was starkly different from the factory floor. It demanded punctuality, precision, and a different kind of discipline. For my father, who had spent years mastering the rhythms and physicality of factory work, this was a new frontier— one that required physical agility and mental acumen.

As the years passed, the small administrative office in the factory grew, mirroring the growth of office culture globally. The rise of multinational corporations and the proliferation of consumer goods in the post-war boom led to an increase in administrative tasks like marketing, customer relations, and international communication.

For my father, the shift from manual labor to office work was a career change and a transformative life experience. It opened up opportunities that were previously unimaginable to someone from his modest background. It was a change that brought both prosperity and personal growth, allowing him to provide for his family in ways that factory work never could have.

As the landscape of work continued to evolve during the mid-20th century, the impact of non-AI-based automation became a catalyst for an entirely new approach to workforce readiness and education. The burgeoning demand for a workforce adept in managing and maintaining increasingly complex machinery and later, computer systems, required a radical shift in how individuals were prepared for their careers.

As industries integrated more sophisticated machinery into their production processes, it became evident that the educational systems in place were inadequate to meet the new demands. This gap spurred the development of vocational schools and technical training institutes aimed at equipping individuals with specific skills relevant to operating and troubleshooting modern equipment. These institutions were designed to foster technical acumen and to instill a mindset of continuous learning and adaptability, qualities essential for thriving in an environment of rapid technological change.

The concept of a "prototype" worker emerged, reflecting the ideal profile of employees who could seamlessly integrate into this new industrial framework. This prototype was characterized by a blend of technical knowledge, problem-solving abilities, and a capacity for lifelong learning. Educational programs began to emphasize STEM subjects (Science, Technology, Engineering, and Mathematics), which were crucial for understanding and advancing in a technology-driven workplace.

Training programs were often developed in collaboration with industries to ensure that the curriculum was directly aligned with the skills required on the job. This partnership between educational institutions and businesses ensured that training was pragmatic and directly applicable, reducing the gap between education and employment. Apprenticeships also saw a resurgence, offering hands-on experience and a direct pathway from education to employment, which was particularly effective in sectors like manufacturing, automotive, and later, computing.

Furthermore, the rise of non-AI automation required a new breed of managers and strategists. Business schools began to incorporate courses on operations management, industrial logistics, and organizational behavior, which were crucial for overseeing automated processes and ensuring that human resources were effectively aligned with technological capabilities.

This period also marked the beginning of what would later become known as "corporate training programs." Companies invested in continuous training for their employees, recognizing that the rapid pace of technological advancement required a workforce that could evolve alongside the machines they operated. These programs aimed to keep employees updated with the latest technological advancements and methodologies, ensuring the company's competitive edge in the market.

As the 20th century progressed, the focus of readiness and education shifted increasingly toward integrating technology with human skills. The groundwork laid during this era set the stage for the later adoption of computer technology and eventually, the seamless integration of AI into the workplace. The educational reforms and the concept of the prototyped worker developed during this time highlighted a fundamental truth that remains relevant: adaptability is as crucial as technical skill in an ever-evolving job market.

In essence, the response to non-AI-based automation during the mid-20th century was not just about equipping people with the skills to handle new technologies, but also about preparing them to be agile learners and versatile workers, capable of navigating the complexities of modern industries. This era fundamentally reshaped the relationship between education, work, and technology, a relationship that continues to evolve to this day.

As the gears of industry turned and non-AI-based automation became more entrenched, the work environment and societal norms surrounding employment also began to shift significantly. The rise of the 9 to 5 job as the standard work arrangement emerged from this period of industrial and economic expansion. This schedule was a byproduct of increased factory and office work, and it was also a reflection of a growing need for structure and predictability in both production schedules and personal lives. This structure allowed workers to have a clear separation between work and home life, which was increasingly important as more families moved into suburban areas, further from industrial city centers.

During this time, the story of my father, like that of many others, was deeply intertwined with these broader changes. As he adapted to his role in the new automated processes of the textile factory, he also found himself dealing with a changing landscape of worker's rights and industrial relations.

The establishment of the 9 to 5 work standard was closely linked to the rise of worker's syndicates and labor unions, which gained considerable influence during this period. Labor unions became more prominent, advocating for workers' rights, fair wages, reasonable hours, and safer working conditions. These efforts were crucial in humanizing the burgeoning industrial machine of the time, ensuring that workers were not merely cogs in a vast factory wheel but recognized as human beings deserving of respect and dignity.

Syndicates and unions often negotiated with employers on behalf of their members, leading to the development of more formalized employment contracts and the introduction of benefits such as paid vacation, sick leave, and health insurance. These negotiations were sometimes tense and could lead to strikes or labor stoppages, but they also led to significant progress in labor laws and regulations.

Government involvement in labor issues became more pronounced during this era. Inspired by the rising power of unions and increasing public awareness of labor issues, governments began to enact laws and regulations to protect workers. These laws covered a wide range of issues, from minimum wage standards to safety regulations in the workplace. In countries across Europe and North America, these legal frameworks began to shape a more formalized and humane working environment.

For my father, these changes were tangible. The factory where he worked started to implement these new standards, transforming his role and also his rights as a worker. He witnessed firsthand the impact of these systemic changes. His hours became more regular, his pay became more reliable, and the conditions under which he worked improved significantly. Moreover, his engagement with the factory's worker syndicate provided him with a sense of belonging, empowering him to advocate for himself and his colleagues.

As my father's story unfolded against this backdrop of technological and regulatory change, it highlighted the interconnected evolution of work, worker rights, and workplace norms. The nine-to-five job, once a novel concept, became a standard, reflecting broader societal shifts toward regularity and balance in the workforce. The journey from manual labor to automated processes, accompanied by an increase in worker protections and rights, set the stage for the later technological revolutions that would continue to shape the nature of work through the 1980s and beyond.

This integration of technology, regulation, and worker rights not only transformed industries but also deeply affected the lives of countless individuals like my father, who navigated these changes with resilience and foresight. His story is proof of the adaptability of the human spirit in the face of profound change, providing a personal lens through which to view these broader historical movements.

Fast forwarding to the 1980s, when I was a curious 10-year-old boy, my fascination was piqued by how miniature people appeared to be omnipresent in many homes, all contained within a tube box—the television. In our neighborhood, which was graced unevenly by the future's arrival, I recall a neighbor, a teacher from a well-off family, who would invite nearly everyone around to watch TV programs at her house. Initially, I don't remember seeing advertisements interrupting the shows, but soon, the commercial breaks became frequent, prompting my young mind to ponder the necessity of advertising products through this magical medium.

Even as a child, I speculated that the commercials on our neighbor's television might differ from those on others', reflecting the diverse tastes of different viewers. This early observation hinted at the personalized marketing strategies that would become prevalent in the future. As television technology evolved from its mechanical roots in the early 1920s, who could have envisioned the myriad of jobs it would spawn? From creating short TV scenarios and advertisements to the roles of cameramen and TV studio workers, the industry expanded far beyond the simple act of broadcasting.

Television, for me, was a window to the world—a magical portal— that presented entertainment and glimpses into different cultures, ideas, and innovations. The spread of television across the globe during the late 20th century mirrored broader technological and economic shifts. It played a pivotal role in shaping public opinion, cultural norms, and even political landscapes across diverse societies.

By the late 1980s and into the 1990s, the television industry had become a cornerstone of the global economy, influencing everything from the advertising industry to consumer behavior. The introduction of cable TV and later, satellite television, expanded the reach and granularity of content delivery, catering to an ever-more segmented audience with specialized channels and programs and guess what: specialized publicity.

As I reflect on this era, it's evident that television was a lot more than just an entertainment medium; it was a significant catalyst for economic and social transformation which helped how the concept of work continued to evolve. It created jobs within the direct sphere of broadcasting and also in ancillary sectors such as electronic manufacturing, advertising, and content creation. The economic ripple effects were profound, with television sets becoming a staple in households worldwide, driving consumer electronics innovation and shaping the early days of the digital revolution.

In understanding the transformative impact of television, we see a precursor to the digital disruptions that would follow with the emergence of the internet and digital media. Just as television redefined entertainment and communication in the 20th century, the digital age would go on to reshape these territories in even more radical ways, setting the stage for the future of work in media, technology, and beyond. This progression from a simple box in the living room to a global industry underscores the dynamic nature of technological innovation and its far-reaching implications on work and society.

As the calendar turned to the new millennium, the pace of technological innovation and globalization accelerated, reshaping industries and the nature of work in profound ways. This era saw the introduction of the internet as a ubiquitous force, transforming how businesses operated and how individuals interacted with the world.

For my father, who had already navigated several waves of industrial change, the 2000s presented both new challenges and opportunities. By this time, he was nearing the end of his career, but the lessons he had learned about adaptability and continuous learning were as relevant as ever. The factory where he worked had evolved dramatically, incorporating more advanced computer systems and automated processes. My father, always keen to stay ahead, took every opportunity to learn about these new technologies, attending training sessions and learning from younger colleagues who were more familiar with the digital world.

The global economy was now deeply interconnected, with supply chains spanning continents and information flowing at the speed of light. The rise of e-commerce giants like Amazon and the proliferation of internet services reshaped consumer behavior and created entirely new industries. In this rapidly changing landscape, my father saw the value of his adaptability and resilience. While many of his peers chose to retire, he continued to find ways to contribute, mentoring younger workers and sharing his wealth of experience.

Meanwhile, I was already into this brave new world as a freshly minted computer engineer for a few years. The technology I worked with was far more advanced than anything my father had encountered at the start of his career. The dot-com boom had given rise to an explosion of startups, each vying to be the next big thing. Silicon Valley became synonymous with innovation, attracting talent from around the globe.

I was struck by how different the workplace had become. Open-plan offices replaced cubicles, fostering collaboration and creativity. Remote work started to gain acceptance, thanks to high-speed internet and communication tools like email and video conferencing. The concept of a 9-to-5 job was evolving, with flexible hours and project-based work becoming more common.

For my father, these changes were both astonishing and inspiring. He marveled at how quickly technology had advanced and how it had opened up new possibilities. We often talked about the differences between his early days in the factory and my experiences in the tech industry. He was particularly fascinated by the way companies like Google and Apple were not just workplaces but campuses, offering amenities like gyms, cafeterias, and even nap pods to keep employees happy and productive. He was clearly astonished by those huge campus concepts that he even could not dream about in the past.

In the 2000s, the rise of digital technologies also meant that traditional industries had to adapt or risk becoming obsolete. Manufacturing processes became increasingly automated, with robotics playing a significant role. The rise of the internet meant that information was no longer siloed within organizations but was accessible to anyone with a connection. This democratization of knowledge led to more informed consumers and a more competitive marketplace.

My father, who had spent a lifetime adapting to change, saw the writing on the wall one more time. He encouraged me to embrace these new technologies and to never stop learning. His advice was invaluable as I navigated the fast-paced world of tech, where the only constant was change. The skills I developed as a computer engineer were in high demand, and I found myself working on projects that my father could only have dreamed of.

My father passed away in 2011, leaving behind a legacy of resilience and adaptability that had guided him through numerous industrial changes. His journey, from operating early textile machines to mentoring younger workers in the digital age, remained a source of inspiration as I continued my career in the IT industry.

By the time of his passing, the world of work was already undergoing significant transformations. The IT sector, in particular, was at the forefront of these changes, revolutionizing how we defined the workplace. The traditional office environment was slowly being replaced by more flexible arrangements. High-speed internet and advancements in communication technology-enabled remote work, allowing employees to collaborate from different corners of the globe.

Freelancing platforms began to emerge, redefining the nature of employment. Websites like Upwork and Freelancer provided a marketplace where individuals could offer their skills to a global audience, bypassing the traditional employer-employee relationship. This shift empowered people to take control of their careers, offering flexibility and opportunities that were previously unimaginable. It was a world where one's skills, rather than one's location, became the currency of work.

As I experienced this evolving landscape, I saw firsthand how these changes were shaping the future of work. The rigid structures of the past were giving way to a more fluid, dynamic approach. Companies began to prioritize outcomes over physical presence, focusing on what employees could deliver rather than where they were located. This shift both increased productivity and allowed for a better work-life balance, a concept that had eluded many for decades.

Then, in 2020, the world was hit by the COVID-19 pandemic. This global crisis acted as a catalyst, accelerating the adoption of remote work and digital collaboration at an unprecedented pace. Offices around the world emptied as lockdowns and social distancing measures were implemented, pushing businesses to adapt quickly or risk collapse.

The pandemic underscored the viability of remote work, proving that many jobs could be performed just as effectively, if not more so, from home. Companies invested heavily in digital infrastructure to support this new way of working, and employees adapted to virtual meetings, digital project management tools, and online collaboration platforms. The traditional office, once seen as essential, became optional for many roles.

Freelancing platforms saw a surge in activity as people sought new ways to earn a living amid economic uncertainty. The gig economy expanded, with more individuals offering their services on a project basis, leveraging their specialized skill sets. This trend highlighted the growing importance of skills-based work, where the ability to deliver results mattered more than the specifics of one's employment status.

As the dust settled, it became clear that the pandemic had permanently altered the landscape of work. Remote work was no longer a temporary solution but a permanent fixture for many businesses. The concept of a "workplace" had evolved to include home offices, coworking spaces, and any location with a stable internet connection. Global collaboration became the norm, breaking down geographical barriers and enabling diverse teams to work together seamlessly.

Now, we stand on the threshold of a new era, one that is already being shaped and dominated by AI. The precise trajectory of this evolution remains uncertain, and the pace of change can be unpredictable. However, there is no doubt that AI will profoundly impact how people work, collaborate, and navigate the job market.

AI is poised to create new job opportunities while simultaneously phasing out certain roles and transforming others. A report[1] by the World Economic Forum predicts that by 2025, AI and automation will displace approximately 85 million jobs but also create 97 million new ones across various industries. This shift underscores the dual nature of technological advancement: while some traditional roles may diminish, new opportunities will arise, requiring workers to adapt and acquire new skills.

The impact of AI on collaboration is equally significant. AI-powered tools and platforms facilitate seamless communication and coordination across global teams, enhancing productivity and innovation. These technologies enable real-time language translation, predictive analytics, and automated project management, making it easier for diverse groups to work together effectively.

One of the most profound changes AI brings is the shift in how we define work itself. The traditional concept of a "job" is evolving into something more fluid and dynamic. Instead of rigid job descriptions, we are moving toward a model where skill sets take precedence. This shift raises fundamental questions about the nature of employment: Will work be organized around individuals holding specific jobs, or will it be defined by tasks that require a combination of skills from multiple people?

Research from the McKinsey Global Institute[2] suggests that by 2030, as many as 375 million workers worldwide may need to switch occupational categories due to automation and AI. This change emphasizes the importance of lifelong learning and the ability to continuously update one's skill set to remain relevant in the job market.

The gig economy, already growing before the pandemic, is likely to expand further as AI enables more precise matching of skills to tasks. Freelance platforms will increasingly rely on AI to connect workers with short-term projects, making it easier for individuals to offer their expertise on a temporary basis. This model provides flexibility for workers and allows companies to access specialized skills on demand.

As we walk through this new era, it is crucial to explore how AI will redefine what constitutes a job. Will it be an individual's responsibility, or will it be a collection of tasks distributed among a network of skilled professionals? The answer to this question will shape the future of work, influencing everything from job training and education to organizational structures and labor laws.

Reflecting on these changes, I often think about my father's journey and how he would have marveled at the flexibility and opportunities available today. His life was a proof of the importance of adaptability, a lesson that remains crucial as we continue to deal with and explore the ever-changing world of work.

The transition from traditional employment to a more flexible, skills-based approach represents a profound shift in how we think about work. It emphasizes the value of continuous learning and the ability to adapt to new technologies and environments. As we move forward, the lessons from the past, combined with the innovations of the present, will guide us in shaping a future where work is more dynamic, inclusive, and fulfilling for everyone.

Economic Transformations Triggered by Technological Advancements

The story of economic progress is inextricably linked to the history of technological advancements. From the earliest human innovations to the complex digital technologies of today, each leap forward in technology has triggered profound economic transformations, reshaping industries, labor markets, and societal structures.

The first major technological breakthrough came with the Agricultural Revolution around 10,000 BC. The domestication of plants and animals transformed human societies from nomadic hunter-gatherers to settled agriculturalists. This shift allowed for the cultivation of surplus food, which in turn supported population growth and the development of complex societies. The surplus generated by improved farming techniques led to the creation of new professions and the division of labor, laying the groundwork for economic specialization and trade.

Fast forward to the 18th century, the Industrial Revolution marked a pivotal era in economic history. Originating in Britain, this period saw the transition from manual labor to mechanized production, driven by inventions such as the steam engine, Spinning Jenny, and power loom. These innovations significantly increased productivity and efficiency in industries like textile, iron, and coal mining.

The impact of mechanization on the economy was multifaceted. Firstly, it reduced the cost of goods, making them more accessible to a broader population and stimulating consumer demand. Secondly, it catalyzed urbanization, as people migrated from rural areas to cities in search of factory jobs. This urban growth spurred the development of infrastructure and new markets. Thirdly, the rise of factories and mass production altered the labor market, creating a need for a large workforce to operate machinery, which in turn led to the rise of the working class and new social dynamics.

The late 19th and early 20th centuries heralded the Second Industrial Revolution, characterized by rapid advancements in electrification, telecommunication, and transportation. The introduction of electricity revolutionized industries by providing a reliable and efficient source of power, leading to the electrification of factories and homes. This era also saw the advent of the telephone and telegraph, which transformed communication, enabling businesses to operate more effectively and fostering global trade networks.

Technological innovations in transportation, such as the internal combustion engine and the automobile, further revolutionized the economy. They facilitated the movement of goods and people over greater distances with unprecedented speed and efficiency, contributing to the growth of suburban areas and the expansion of markets.

The mid-20th century introduced the Digital Revolution, a transformative period marked by the development of computers, the internet, and information technology. The invention of the transistor and the microprocessor laid the foundation for modern computing, while the launch of the World Wide Web in the 1990s opened up new frontiers for communication and commerce.

Computing technology revolutionized industries by automating tasks, improving data management, and enabling sophisticated data analysis. This automation increased productivity across sectors, from manufacturing to services. The internet, in particular, reshaped the economy by facilitating e-commerce, reducing transaction costs, and creating new business models like online marketplaces and digital platforms.

Technological advancements have also driven globalization, integrating economies and markets worldwide. Innovations in transportation and communication have made it easier for businesses to operate on a global scale, outsourcing production and services to countries with comparative advantages. This integration has led to increased trade, investment, and economic interdependence among nations.

The rise of the knowledge economy, fueled by information technology, has shifted the focus from physical goods to intellectual assets. Industries such as software development, biotechnology, and financial services have become key drivers of economic growth, emphasizing the importance of education, research, and innovation.

Today, we stand on the brink of another transformative period, driven by automation and AI. These technologies are poised to revolutionize the economy once again, offering unprecedented opportunities for productivity gains and economic growth. Automation is already reshaping industries by performing tasks that were previously labor-intensive, while AI is enabling new levels of efficiency and innovation.

The integration of AI into various sectors, from healthcare to finance, is expected to create new job opportunities while also displacing some traditional roles. The challenge lies in managing this transition, ensuring that the workforce is equipped with the necessary skills to thrive in a rapidly evolving job market.

As we delve into the transformative effects of technological advancements on the economy, it is essential to explore four central themes that have continually reshaped our understanding of work and economic growth: automation, productivity, abundance, and future job landscapes. These themes are interconnected, each influencing and amplifying the others, creating a complex tapestry of economic evolution and societal change.

Automation: The Engine of Efficiency

Automation refers to the use of technology to perform tasks that were once carried out by humans. This concept has evolved significantly over time, from the mechanized looms of the Industrial Revolution to the sophisticated AI systems of today. Automation is driven by the pursuit of efficiency, aiming to reduce labor costs, increase production speed, and enhance precision.

The impact of automation on the economy is profound. By automating repetitive and mundane tasks, businesses can redirect human labor toward more complex and creative endeavors. This shift boosts productivity and drives innovation, as workers are freed to focus on problem-solving and strategic thinking. However, automation also presents challenges, such as job displacement and the need for workforce retraining.

Productivity: The Key to Economic Growth

Productivity measures the efficiency of production, typically expressed as the output per unit of input. Technological advancements, particularly automation, have been pivotal in driving productivity gains. From assembly lines to robotic manufacturing, each leap in technology has enabled businesses to produce more with less, reducing costs and increasing the availability of goods.

Higher productivity leads to economic growth by allowing businesses to scale operations and meet increasing consumer demand. It also contributes to higher wages and improved standards of living, as more efficient production processes translate into cheaper goods and services. The productivity gains achieved through automation are a critical component of sustained economic growth and competitiveness in the global market.

Abundance: From Scarcity to Plentitude

The concept of abundance is closely tied to the effects of automation and productivity. Historically, economies were characterized by scarcity, with limited resources and goods available to meet human needs. However, technological advancements have shifted this paradigm, creating an era of abundance where goods and services are more widely accessible.

Automation has played a significant role in this transition by lowering production costs and increasing output. As a result, a broader range of products becomes available at lower prices, democratizing access to once-scarce resources. This shift toward abundance has transformed consumer behavior, driving demand for a diverse array of goods and fostering economic growth.

The implications of abundance extend beyond consumer markets. It also affects the nature of work and societal structures. In a world where basic needs are easily met, individuals have more freedom to pursue personal interests and creative endeavors, potentially reshaping the very notion of work.

Future Job Landscapes: Navigating the New World of Work

As we look to the future, the landscape of work is poised for a dramatic transformation. Automation and AI are expected to redefine job roles and create new employment opportunities while rendering some traditional jobs obsolete. This evolution will require a flexible and adaptable workforce, capable of acquiring new skills and navigating a rapidly changing job market.

Future job landscapes will likely be characterized by increased emphasis on specialized skill sets and collaborative work. The rise of freelancing and gig economies illustrates this shift, with platforms enabling individuals to offer their expertise on a project basis. This model allows for greater flexibility and autonomy but also necessitates continuous learning and skill development.

The integration of AI into various industries will create demand for new types of jobs, such as AI trainers, data scientists, and robot maintenance specialists. These roles will require a blend of technical knowledge and human creativity, emphasizing the importance of interdisciplinary education and lifelong learning.

Automation has long been a catalyst for economic growth, fundamentally transforming industries and enhancing productivity. By delegating repetitive and routine tasks to machines, automation allows human labor to be redirected toward more complex and value-added activities. This shift not only boosts efficiency but also drives innovation and competitiveness in the global market. To understand the economic impact of automation, it is essential to explore how it increases productivity and reshapes industries.

The concept of automation can be traced back to the Industrial Revolution, which marked the first significant wave of mechanization. The introduction of steam-powered machinery, such as the steam engine and mechanized looms, revolutionized production processes in industries like textile, iron, and coal mining. These innovations enabled factories to produce goods at unprecedented speeds and scales, laying the foundation for modern industrial economies.

For instance, the power loom, invented by Edmund Cartwright in 1785, dramatically increased the efficiency of textile production. It reduced the time and labor required to weave cloth, leading to a surge in output and a decline in production costs. This mechanization not only transformed the textile industry but also spurred economic growth by making textiles more affordable and accessible to a broader population.

The late 19th and early 20th centuries saw the emergence of the Second Industrial Revolution, characterized by the widespread adoption of electricity and the development of mass production techniques. The assembly line, popularized by Henry Ford in the early 20th century, epitomized this era. By standardizing and streamlining the production process, the assembly line significantly increased productivity in the automotive industry.

Henry Ford's implementation of the moving assembly line in 1913 reduced the time it took to assemble a Model T from over 12 hours to just 93 minutes. This leap in productivity allowed Ford to lower the price of the Model T, making automobiles more accessible to the average consumer and revolutionizing transportation. The principles of mass production were soon adopted by other industries, further driving economic growth and industrial expansion.

The mid-20th century introduced the Digital Revolution, which brought about a new wave of automation through the development of computers and information technology. The invention of the transistor in 1947 and the microprocessor in the 1970s paved the way for modern computing, enabling the automation of complex tasks and data processing.

Computers revolutionized industries by automating administrative tasks, improving data management, and enabling sophisticated data analysis. For example, in the manufacturing sector, Computer Numerical Control (CNC) machines allowed for the precise automation of machining processes, increasing both speed and accuracy. This technological leap both boosted productivity and improved the quality and consistency of manufactured goods.

The internet, which became widely accessible in the 1990s, further enhanced productivity by facilitating global communication and commerce. E-commerce platforms like Amazon and Alibaba leveraged automation to streamline logistics and inventory management, reducing costs and delivery times. This digital infrastructure enabled businesses to scale operations and reach new markets, driving economic growth and innovation.

Today, automation is entering a new phase with the integration of AI and machine learning. These technologies are capable of performing tasks that require cognitive abilities, such as pattern recognition, decision-making, and natural language processing. AI-powered automation is transforming industries ranging from healthcare to finance, creating new opportunities for productivity gains.

In the healthcare sector, for example, AI algorithms can analyze medical images with remarkable accuracy, assisting doctors in diagnosing diseases more quickly and accurately. This both improves patient outcomes and reduces the time and resources required for medical examinations. In finance, AI-driven trading algorithms can process vast amounts of data in real time, optimizing investment strategies and increasing market efficiency.

The economic benefits of automation are multifaceted. By increasing productivity, automation allows businesses to produce more goods and services with the same or fewer inputs. This efficiency translates into lower production costs, enabling companies to offer competitive prices and increase profit margins. The cost savings from automation can be reinvested in research and development, driving further innovation and economic growth.

Additionally, automation can enhance the quality and consistency of products, leading to higher consumer satisfaction and loyalty. In industries where precision and reliability are critical, such as aerospace and pharmaceuticals, automated systems can ensure that products meet stringent quality standards.

Automation also contributes to economic resilience by enabling businesses to adapt to changing market conditions. During periods of high demand, automated systems can scale production quickly, meeting consumer needs without compromising quality. Conversely, during economic downturns, automation allows companies to maintain operations efficiently, reducing the need for drastic workforce reductions.

By automating repetitive and labor-intensive tasks, businesses can significantly cut down on labor expenses. Machines and automated systems can operate continuously without breaks, vacations, or shifts, leading to higher productivity and efficiency.

These reductions in production costs allow businesses to lower the prices of their goods. Cheaper goods mean that more people can afford to buy them, expanding the market and increasing sales volume. This phenomenon is known as *the price elasticity of demand*, where a decrease in price leads to a proportionately larger increase in the quantity demanded.

Lower prices resulting from automation lead to higher consumer demand. When goods become more affordable, a larger segment of the population can purchase them. This increase in demand stimulates further production, creating a positive feedback loop that drives economic growth. To better understand this phenomenon, we can look at several key economic theories that explain why lower prices can have such a significant impact on consumer behavior and overall economic activity.

Economic theories such as the Law of Demand and the Income Effect provide a framework for understanding how automation-driven cost reductions translate into increased consumer demand and broader economic benefits. The Law of Demand, for instance, illustrates the relationship between price decreases and quantity demanded, while the Income Effect explains how consumers' purchasing power expands when prices fall. Together, these principles help elucidate the mechanisms by which automation fuels economic growth.

As a real-world example, we can take consumer electronics. The automation of manufacturing processes for consumer electronics, such as smartphones and computers, has significantly reduced their costs. This has made these technologies accessible to a global market, driving massive demand and continuous innovation in the sector.

The combination of reduced production costs and increased consumer demand drives overall economic growth. As businesses produce more goods to meet rising demand, they require more raw materials, intermediate goods, and services. This creates a ripple effect throughout the economy, benefiting various industries and sectors:

1. Job Creation: While automation can displace certain jobs, it also creates new ones, particularly in sectors related to technology, maintenance, and the development of new products and services. For instance, the rise of the automotive industry created millions of jobs in manufacturing, sales, and maintenance.

2. Investment in Innovation: The profits generated from increased sales and reduced costs can be reinvested in research and development. This investment drives further technological advancements, creating a virtuous cycle of innovation and growth. For example, the semiconductor industry has continuously invested in developing more powerful and efficient microchips, fueling advancements across multiple sectors.

3. *Economic Multiplier Effect:* The increased production and consumption resulting from automation contribute to the economic multiplier effect, where an initial increase in spending leads to a more significant overall increase in economic activity. As workers earn wages from new jobs, they spend more on goods and services, further boosting demand and economic growth.

Over time, the cumulative effects of automation and technological advancements have led to profound structural changes in the economy:

1. *Diversification of Industries:* Automation has enabled the development of new industries and the expansion of existing ones. For example, advancements in automation and robotics have spurred growth in sectors like biotechnology, aerospace, and clean energy.

2. *Globalization:* Technological advancements have facilitated the globalization of production and markets. Companies can now operate supply chains that span the globe, taking advantage of efficiencies and cost savings offered by different regions. This globalization has increased trade and investment flows, contributing to global economic growth.

3. *Consumer Empowerment:* Automation has also empowered consumers by providing them with more choices and better-quality products at lower prices. Enhanced production capabilities and competition have driven innovation, leading to continuous improvements in product features and performance.

From Scarcity to Abundance

The history of human civilization is largely a story of scarcity. For millennia, humans have struggled to produce enough food, clothing, and shelter to meet their basic needs. Resources were limited, and the means of production were labor-intensive and inefficient. This scarcity dictated much of the social and economic structures that developed over time. However, the rise of automation and technological advancements has gradually shifted this paradigm, ushering in an era characterized by the concept of abundance.

Understanding Scarcity

Scarcity refers to the fundamental economic problem of having seemingly unlimited human wants in a world of limited resources. It is the driving force behind many economic theories and practices, dictating how resources are allocated and how value is assigned. Scarcity has historically forced societies to make difficult choices about what to produce, how to produce it, and for whom it is produced.

The Transition to Abundance

Automation, particularly since the Industrial Revolution, has played a pivotal role in transitioning societies from scarcity to abundance. By dramatically increasing productivity and efficiency, automation has enabled the mass production of goods and services at lower costs, making them more accessible to a broader population. This shift can be understood through several key developments:

Mass Production and Lower Costs

1. Industrial Revolution: The mechanization of manufacturing processes during the Industrial Revolution significantly increased the production capacity of industries. Machines such as the Spinning Jenny and the steam engine allowed for the mass production of goods, reducing their cost and making them available to more people.

2. 20th Century Automation: The assembly line and later, computer-controlled manufacturing, further reduced production costs. This led to a proliferation of consumer goods, from automobiles to household appliances, becoming commonplace in many homes.

Technological Advancements and Efficiency

1. Digital Revolution: The introduction of computers and digital technologies in the late 20th century revolutionized industries by automating complex tasks, improving efficiency, and reducing human error. This digital transformation extended beyond manufacturing to services and information industries, further contributing to abundance.

2. AI and Robotics: In the 21st century, AI and robotics have taken automation to new heights. These technologies are capable of performing tasks that require cognitive skills and precision, pushing the boundaries of what can be automated. For example, robotic systems in warehouses can sort and package goods at speeds and accuracies unattainable by human workers.

Defining Abundance

Abundance refers to the condition where goods and services are produced in such quantities that they become readily available to a large segment of the population at low cost. It represents a significant departure from the traditional economic model of scarcity, where limited resources constrain production and availability.

Characteristics of Abundance

1. Wide Availability of Goods and Services: In an abundant economy, basic necessities such as food, clothing, and shelter are produced efficiently and are widely accessible. This reduces the time and effort individuals need to spend on securing these essentials, freeing up resources for other pursuits.

2. Lower Costs and Increased Accessibility: Automation reduces production costs, leading to lower prices for consumers. This makes a wider range of products and services affordable to more people, enhancing their quality of life.

3. Enhanced Quality and Innovation: With automation handling routine tasks, human labor can focus on innovation and improving product quality. This drive for innovation leads to better and more diverse products, further contributing to abundance. The rapid advancements in technology and continuous improvement in product features exemplify this characteristic.

Economic and Social Implications of Abundance

The concept of abundance, often associated with technological advancements and economic prosperity carries profound economic and social implications. As we navigate through an era marked by unprecedented technological proliferation and innovation, understanding these implications becomes critical.

Economically, abundance manifests in several ways, primarily through increased productivity and efficiency. However, the economic implications are not uniformly positive. The proliferation of automation and AI could lead to job displacement in certain industries, creating a divide between those who can adapt to the new technological landscape and those who cannot. This could exacerbate income inequality and lead to economic instability if not managed properly. On the flip side, it also opens up new opportunities for jobs and industries that were previously non-existent, fostering innovation and new economic models. The gig economy, for instance, has emerged as a significant player in the modern economic landscape, providing flexible work opportunities and catering to a global workforce.

Socially, the implications of abundance are equally profound. On one hand, it can lead to greater social equity and improved quality of life. Access to education, healthcare, and information has been revolutionized by technological advances, leading to better outcomes in terms of health, knowledge, and overall well-being. The democratization of information through the internet and digital platforms has empowered individuals, giving them a voice and access to opportunities that were previously out of reach.

Yet, this abundance also brings about social challenges. The digital divide remains a significant issue, where sections of the population, particularly in developing regions, are left behind due to a lack of access to technology. This can lead to a disparity in opportunities and outcomes, further entrenching social inequalities. Additionally, the overwhelming abundance of information can lead to misinformation and societal fragmentation, as seen in the proliferation of fake news and echo chambers on social media platforms.

Moreover, the psychological impact of abundance is a critical aspect to consider. With an abundance of choices and information, individuals can experience decision fatigue and a sense of overwhelm. This paradox of choice can lead to stress and anxiety, as people struggle to navigate the myriad of options available to them. The societal pressure to keep up with the constant flow of new trends and innovations can also contribute to mental health issues.

Future Implications of Abundance

As automation and AI continue to evolve, the concept of abundance will shape the future of work and society in several ways:

1. *Shift in Job Nature and Skills:* As routine tasks are increasingly automated, the demand for jobs that require creative, strategic, and interpersonal skills will rise. Education and training systems will need to adapt to prepare individuals for these new roles.

2. *Universal Basic Services:* In an abundant economy, the idea of universal basic services, where essential goods and services are provided free or at minimal cost to all citizens, may become feasible. This could include healthcare, education, and basic income, ensuring a higher quality of life for everyone.

3. Focus on Quality of Life: With the basics of life more easily secured, societies may place greater emphasis on quality of life, well-being, and personal fulfillment. This could lead to a renaissance in arts, culture, and sciences as people pursue their passions and interests.

4. Economic Models and Policies: Policymakers will need to develop new economic models and policies to manage the implications of abundance. This includes addressing income inequality, ensuring fair distribution of resources, and fostering sustainable growth.

The transition from scarcity to abundance, driven by technological advancements and automation, fundamentally transforms the nature of work and job availability. As economies move from models based on scarcity to those driven by abundance, the implications for the workforce are profound and multifaceted.

The impact of abundance on the nature of work is first and foremost a shift in how labor is valued and utilized. In scarcity-driven models, work is primarily about survival and fulfilling basic needs. Jobs are often repetitive and labor-intensive, with workers required to perform manual tasks essential for production. The focus is on efficiency and output, with little room for creativity or innovation. However, as automation increases productivity and reduces the cost of goods and services, the economic landscape begins to change. Basic needs become easier to meet, and the nature of work shifts toward tasks that require higher-order skills, creativity, and strategic thinking.

In an abundance-driven economy, routine and repetitive tasks are increasingly automated, allowing human workers to focus on more complex and fulfilling roles. This shift not only enhances productivity but also increases job satisfaction, as workers engage in tasks that require critical thinking, problem-solving, and innovation. The role of human labor becomes less about performing basic tasks and more about adding value through unique human capabilities that machines cannot easily replicate.

One of the most significant changes brought about by abundance is the increased availability of flexible and remote work opportunities. With the rise of digital technologies and high-speed internet, geographic location becomes less relevant. Workers can collaborate with colleagues from around the world, participate in global projects, and access job opportunities that were previously unavailable. This shift has been accelerated by the COVID-19 pandemic, which demonstrated the viability of remote work on a large scale. Companies have realized the benefits of flexible work arrangements, including reduced overhead costs, access to a broader talent pool, and increased employee satisfaction.

Freelancing platforms and the gig economy further exemplify the impact of abundance on job availability. These platforms enable individuals to offer their skills on a project-by-project basis, providing flexibility and autonomy. Workers can choose projects that align with their interests and expertise, leading to a more dynamic and diverse job market. This model benefits both workers, who enjoy greater freedom and variety, and employers, who can access specialized skills as needed without the long-term commitment of traditional employment.

As we look to the future, the job market is likely to see the emergence of new roles and industries driven by technological advancements and the continued shift toward abundance. Speculations on future job markets suggest several key trends:

1. *AI and Robotics Specialists:* As AI and robotics continue to evolve, there will be a growing demand for specialists who can develop, maintain, and improve these technologies. Roles such as

AI trainers, robotic process automation (RPA) developers, and machine learning engineers will become increasingly important.

2. *Digital and Data Analysts:* The abundance of data generated by digital platforms and connected devices will require skilled analysts who can interpret and leverage this information. Data scientists, big data analysts, and cybersecurity experts will be essential for extracting insights and ensuring data security.

3. *Sustainability and Green Technology Experts:* With growing awareness of environmental issues and the need for sustainable practices, jobs in green technology and sustainability will rise. Roles such as renewable energy technicians, environmental consultants, and sustainability coordinators will be critical in addressing climate change and promoting eco-friendly practices.

4. *Healthcare and Biotechnology Professionals:* Advances in medical technology and biotechnology will create new opportunities in healthcare. Jobs such as genetic counselors, bioinformatics specialists, and telemedicine practitioners will be vital in improving healthcare delivery and personalized medicine.

5. *Creative and Cultural Roles:* As automation takes over routine tasks, there will be more room for creative and cultural roles. Artists, content creators, virtual reality designers, and experience managers will play a significant role in shaping the cultural landscape and providing unique human experiences.

6. *Education and Lifelong Learning Facilitators:* The shift toward a knowledge-based economy will necessitate continuous learning and skill development. Educators, curriculum designers, and e-learning specialists will be essential in providing the training and education needed for the workforce to adapt to new technologies and job requirements.

7. Remote Work Coordinators and Digital Nomad Advisors: With the rise of remote work, there will be a need for professionals who can manage and optimize remote work environments. Remote work coordinators, digital nomad advisors, and virtual team managers will help organizations and individuals navigate the challenges and opportunities of working from anywhere.

The transition from scarcity-driven work models to abundance-driven lifestyles also raises important questions about income distribution and economic equality. As automation increases productivity and reduces the need for certain types of labor, there is a risk of widening income inequality. Policymakers and business leaders must address these challenges by developing inclusive economic policies that ensure the benefits of abundance are shared broadly across society. This could include measures such as universal basic income, progressive taxation, and investment in public services and education.

Exploring the Idea of AI Taking Over Most Jobs

The rapid advancement of AI has sparked considerable debate about its potential to take over a significant portion of jobs currently performed by humans. AI, with its ability to learn, adapt, and perform complex tasks, is already transforming industries and redefining the nature of work. From autonomous vehicles to intelligent chatbots, AI technologies are capable of performing tasks that were once thought to be uniquely human.

The automation of routine and repetitive tasks by AI is well documented. In manufacturing, AI-driven robots are assembling products with precision and efficiency. In finance, AI algorithms are processing transactions and managing investments with minimal human intervention. Even in creative fields, AI is being used to generate art, music, and literature. This trend raises questions about the future of human labor and the potential for AI to replace jobs across various sectors. Will there be a time when AI will take over all the jobs?

Historical Comparison to Ancient Societies

To understand the implications of AI taking over most jobs, it is helpful to draw historical comparisons. One pertinent analogy is with ancient societies, such as those of ancient Greece and Rome, where much of the labor was performed by slaves. In these societies, slaves were responsible for a wide range of tasks, from agriculture and household chores to skilled trades and administrative work. This allowed the free citizens to engage in activities such as politics, philosophy, art, and leisure.

The reliance on slave labor in ancient societies created a dichotomy between those who worked out of necessity and those who were free to pursue intellectual and cultural endeavors. While the comparison is not perfect—slavery being a fundamentally inhumane institution—the analogy helps illustrate how the delegation of labor can free up time for other pursuits. In a future where AI performs many of the tasks currently done by humans, we might see a similar shift, where people are liberated from mundane work and can focus on more fulfilling activities.

The Potential for Human Leisure and Personal Fulfillment

The idea that AI could take over most jobs raises intriguing possibilities for human society. If AI and automation can handle the majority of routine and repetitive tasks, humans may have more time to focus on leisure, creativity, and personal fulfillment. This shift could lead to a renaissance of human potential, where individuals are free to pursue their passions, engage in lifelong learning, and contribute to society in more meaningful ways.

The concept of a leisure-oriented society is not new. Thinkers like John Maynard Keynes predicted that technological advancements would eventually reduce the need for human labor, leading to a future where people work less and enjoy more leisure time. In his 1930 essay *"Economic Possibilities for Our Grandchildren,"* Keynes envisioned a world where technological progress would allow people to work as little as 15 hours a week, with the rest of their time devoted to personal interests and social activities.

In such a society, the definition of work could expand beyond traditional economic activities to include a broader range of pursuits that contribute to individual and collective well-being. Volunteer work, caregiving, artistic creation, and community engagement could be valued as essential components of a thriving society. The shift toward a leisure-oriented society could also promote mental and physical health, as people have more time to rest, exercise, and engage in activities that bring them joy.

As we walk toward the transition into an era dominated by AI, it is crucial for both individuals and societies to develop strategies to adapt effectively. The rapid pace of technological change demands a proactive approach to ensure that the benefits of AI are maximized while minimizing potential disruptions to the workforce and economy.

The Role of Continuous Learning and Upskilling

One of the most effective strategies for individuals to thrive in an AI-driven future is the commitment to continuous learning and upskilling. As AI and automation transform job requirements, the skills that were once sufficient may no longer be relevant. Embracing a mindset of lifelong learning is essential to remain competitive in the job market.

1. Adaptability: Workers must be willing to adapt to new technologies and processes. This involves staying informed about industry trends and being open to acquiring new skills that align with emerging job opportunities.

2. *Skill Development Programs*: Governments, educational institutions, and businesses should collaborate to provide accessible and relevant training programs. These programs should focus on both technical skills, such as programming and data analysis, and soft skills, such as critical thinking, creativity, and EQ.

3. *Online Learning Platforms*: The proliferation of online learning platforms offers unprecedented opportunities for individuals to learn at their own pace and convenience. Platforms like Coursera, edX, and Udacity provide courses on a wide range of subjects, often in partnership with leading universities and companies.

4. *Industry-Specific Training*: Tailored training programs that address the specific needs of various industries can help workers transition into new roles more smoothly. For example, manufacturing workers could benefit from training in robotics and automation, while healthcare professionals might focus on AI applications in medical diagnostics.

The Importance of Flexible Economic Policies to Support Transitions

To ensure a smooth transition into an AI-dominated economy, it is essential for governments to implement flexible and forward-thinking economic policies. These policies should aim to support workers during periods of change and promote inclusive economic growth.

1. *Social Safety Nets*: Strengthening social safety nets can provide a safety cushion for individuals displaced by automation. Programs such as unemployment insurance, universal basic income (UBI), and social assistance can help mitigate the financial impact of job loss and provide stability during the transition period.

2. Tax Incentives for Training: Governments can incentivize businesses to invest in employee training and development through tax credits and subsidies. By reducing the financial burden on companies, these incentives can encourage more widespread adoption of upskilling initiatives.

3. Labor Market Flexibility: Policies that promote labor market flexibility can help workers transition between jobs more easily. This includes measures such as portable benefits, which allow workers to retain health insurance and retirement savings as they move between employers or engage in gig work. We will be looking into this in more detail later in the book.

4. Investment in Innovation: Governments should invest in research and development to drive innovation and create new industries. Public funding for scientific research, technology incubators, and innovation hubs can stimulate economic growth and generate new job opportunities.

5. Inclusive Economic Policies: Ensuring that the benefits of AI and automation are broadly shared requires inclusive economic policies. Progressive taxation, wealth redistribution, and investment in public goods and services can help reduce inequality and ensure that all members of society benefit from technological advancements.

Fostering a Culture of Innovation and Resilience

Beyond individual efforts and government policies, fostering a culture of innovation and resilience is crucial for navigating the AI-driven future. This involves creating environments where creativity and experimentation are encouraged, and where failure is seen as a learning opportunity rather than a setback.

1. *Corporate Innovation*: Businesses should prioritize innovation by creating cultures that encourage experimentation and reward creative problem-solving. This can involve setting aside resources for research and development, as well as establishing innovation teams or labs dedicated to exploring new ideas.

2. *Public-Private Partnerships*: Collaboration between the public and private sectors can drive innovation and address societal challenges. Public-private partnerships can leverage the strengths of both sectors to develop solutions that benefit the broader community.

3. *Resilience Training*: Building resilience is essential for individuals and organizations facing rapid change. Resilience training programs can help workers develop the mental and emotional strength to navigate uncertainty and adapt to new circumstances.

Ethical Considerations and Societal Implications

While the potential benefits of an AI-driven workforce are significant, there are also important ethical considerations and societal implications to address. One of the primary concerns is the displacement of workers and the resulting economic inequality. As AI takes over more jobs, there is a risk that those who are unable to adapt to the new technological landscape will be left behind, exacerbating existing inequalities.

To mitigate these risks, it is essential to develop policies and programs that support workers during the transition to an AI-driven economy. This could include initiatives such as:

1. *Reskilling and Education*: Investing in education and training programs to help workers acquire new skills that are in demand in the AI-driven economy. Lifelong learning should become the norm, with accessible opportunities for continuous skill development.

To truly prepare for the future, we must begin investing in education and training from childhood, ensuring that the next generation is equipped with the skills and mindset needed to navigate and thrive amidst these transformative changes.

Imagine a world where education systems are redesigned to cultivate creativity, critical thinking, and adaptability from the earliest stages of learning. Instead of the traditional rote learning model, classrooms become dynamic environments where problem-solving and innovative thinking are at the forefront. Children as young as preschool age are introduced to the basics of coding and logical reasoning through engaging, playful activities that stimulate their curiosity and foster a love for learning.

As students progress through their educational journey, the curriculum evolves to include more advanced concepts related to AI, data science, and digital literacy. In middle school, students might participate in hands-on projects that involve programming simple robots, analyzing data sets, or developing basic AI algorithms. These experiences would help build technical skills and encourage teamwork, project management, and the ability to iterate and improve upon their work.

High schools and secondary education institutions become incubators for future talent, offering specialized tracks in AI, robotics, cybersecurity, and other emerging fields. Partnerships with tech companies and higher education institutions provide students with access to cutting-edge technology and real-world applications of their learning. Internships and mentorship programs connect students with industry professionals, allowing them to gain practical experience and insights into the working world.

Beyond technical skills, an emphasis on lifelong learning is instilled from a young age. Students are encouraged to view education as a continuous journey rather than a finite process. This mindset prepares them to adapt to new technologies and industry shifts throughout their careers. Schools and communities support this culture of lifelong learning by providing resources and opportunities for ongoing education and professional development.

In this vision of the future, education systems also prioritize soft skills that are increasingly valuable in an AI-driven world. Communication, EQ, creativity, and ethical reasoning are integrated into the curriculum, ensuring that students are technically proficient as well as capable of understanding the complex social and ethical dimensions of new technologies. Collaborative projects, debates, and interdisciplinary courses help students develop these essential skills, making them well-rounded individuals ready to tackle the challenges of the future.

As we invest in this comprehensive approach to education, we are not just preparing children to fill future job roles; we are empowering them to be the innovators, leaders, and thinkers who will shape the next wave of technological advancement. By embedding the principles of reskilling and continuous learning from childhood, we create a resilient workforce capable of thriving in an ever-changing economic landscape.

2. Social Safety Nets: Strengthening social safety nets to provide financial support to those displaced by automation. Universal basic income (UBI) is one such proposal that aims to ensure a basic standard of living for all, regardless of employment status.

3. Ethical AI Development: Ensuring that AI technologies are developed and deployed ethically, with consideration for their impact on society. This includes addressing issues such as algorithmic bias, data privacy, and the potential for AI to be used in harmful ways.

4. *Inclusive Economic Policies:* Designing economic policies that promote inclusive growth and ensure that the benefits of automation are shared broadly. This could involve progressive taxation, wealth redistribution, and investment in public goods and services.

Another ethical consideration is the potential loss of purpose and meaning for individuals whose jobs are replaced by AI. Work has long been a source of identity, purpose, and social connection for many people. As AI takes over more tasks, it is important to find new ways for individuals to find fulfillment and meaning in their lives. This could involve redefining what it means to contribute to society and recognizing the value of activities beyond traditional employment.

In addition, there are concerns about the concentration of power and wealth in the hands of those who control AI technologies. If the benefits of AI-driven productivity are not widely distributed, there is a risk of creating a new class of AI elites who wield significant economic and political power. Ensuring that AI is developed and used for the common good will require collaborative efforts between governments, businesses, and civil society.

Navigating the New Global Economy: Jobs, Job Markets, and Work

Introduction: The Interconnected Global Economy

The global economy has become increasingly interconnected, and this integration profoundly influences job markets and the nature of work. Global dynamics, shaped by technological advancements, shifting economic powers, geopolitical events, and changing societal norms, create a complex environment where job markets are constantly evolving.

Technological advancements play a pivotal role in shaping global job markets. The rise of digital platforms, automation, AI, and e-commerce has transformed industries and created new job opportunities. These technologies facilitate international trade and commerce, enabling businesses to operate on a global scale and access new markets. As companies expand their operations internationally, they create a demand for a diverse set of skills, leading to the creation of new job roles that did not exist a few decades ago. For instance, the growth of e-commerce has spurred demand for logistics managers, digital marketers, data analysts, and IT professionals.

The shift in global economic power is another critical factor influencing job markets. Emerging markets, particularly in Asia, Africa, and Latin America, have seen rapid economic growth, altering the global economic landscape. Countries like China and India have become significant players in the global economy, contributing to job creation both domestically and internationally. As these economies grow, they attract foreign investment, leading to the establishment of multinational companies and the creation of jobs. This shift also impacts developed economies, as businesses increasingly look to outsource operations to regions with lower labor costs, thereby affecting job availability and wage levels in their home countries.

Geopolitical events and trends significantly impact global employment and job stability. Trade policies, regional conflicts, and international agreements shape the economic environment in which businesses operate. Trade wars, for example, can disrupt supply chains, leading to job losses in affected industries. Conversely, trade agreements can open up new markets and create job opportunities. Regional conflicts and political instability can deter investment and hamper economic growth, resulting in job losses and reduced economic activity. On the other hand, geopolitical stability and favorable trade policies can foster an environment conducive to business growth and job creation.

The transformation of global supply chains, driven by technological advancements and geopolitical shifts, also impacts job markets. The move toward more resilient and flexible supply chain models requires a workforce with new skills and capabilities. Automation and AI are increasingly integrated into supply chain operations, reducing the need for manual labor but increasing demand for workers skilled in managing and maintaining these technologies. This shift needs a focus on reskilling and upskilling the workforce to meet the demands of the evolving job market.

The rise of remote work is another significant trend shaping global job markets. High-speed internet and digital communication tools have made it possible for employees to work from anywhere in the world. This shift has expanded the global talent pool, allowing companies to hire the best talent regardless of geographical location. Remote work offers flexibility and can lead to increased productivity and job satisfaction. However, it also presents challenges, such as managing a distributed workforce and ensuring data security. The ability to tap into a global talent pool can also lead to increased competition for jobs, as workers from different regions vie for the same positions.

Economic inequality is a growing concern within and between countries, influencing job markets and workforce policies. Technological advancements and globalization have contributed to widening income disparities, as high-skilled workers benefit more from these changes than low-skilled workers. Addressing economic inequality requires targeted policy responses, such as investing in education and training programs to equip workers with the skills needed for the future job market. Social safety nets and progressive taxation can also help mitigate the impact of inequality and ensure that the benefits of economic growth are broadly shared.

Sustainability is becoming increasingly important in the global economy, influencing job creation and economic policies. There is a growing recognition of the need for sustainable practices to address environmental challenges and promote long-term economic stability. This shift toward sustainability creates new job opportunities in green industries, such as renewable energy, waste management, and sustainable agriculture. The Paris Agreement, an international treaty adopted in 2015, plays a crucial role in promoting sustainable employment and guiding economic policies toward a more sustainable future. The Paris Agreement aims to limit global warming to well below 2 degrees Celsius, preferably to 1.5 degrees, compared to pre-industrial levels. It encourages countries to reduce greenhouse gas emissions, invest in renewable energy, and implement policies that support sustainable development. By fostering global cooperation on climate action, the Paris Agreement helps drive the transition to a green economy and the creation of environmentally friendly jobs.

Global dynamics, hence, profoundly influence job markets and the nature of work. Technological advancements, shifts in global economic power, geopolitical events, and the rise of remote work are key factors shaping the employment landscape. Addressing economic inequality and promoting sustainability are essential to creating a more inclusive and stable global economy. As the world continues to evolve, understanding these dynamics and their impact on job markets is crucial for developing strategies that support workers and businesses in navigating the changing economic landscape.

The Ukraine war provides a stark illustration of how global dynamics, particularly geopolitical events, can have far-reaching impacts on job markets and the nature of work, reinforcing the interconnectedness of the global economy. This conflict has disrupted local labor markets as well as created ripple effects across regional and global supply chains, highlighting the intricate web of economic relationships that define our modern world.

The immediate impact of the Ukraine war on local labor markets has been profound. Ukraine is a significant exporter of agricultural products, including wheat and sunflower oil, as well as key industrial materials. The conflict has severely disrupted these industries, leading to reduced production and significant job losses. Factories and farms have been destroyed or repurposed for the war effort, and many workers have been displaced, either fleeing the country or being conscripted into military service. This disruption highlights how local labor markets can be swiftly and drastically affected by geopolitical instability.

The displacement of millions of Ukrainians has created both challenges and opportunities for neighboring countries. As refugees have poured into Poland, Germany, Romania, and other nearby nations, there has been an immediate strain on social services, housing, and infrastructure. However, these countries have also seen an influx of potential workers who can help address local labor shortages, particularly in sectors such as agriculture, construction, and services. This demographic shift required a rapid adjustment in regional labor markets, showcasing the flexibility and resilience needed to accommodate such changes.

Ukraine's role as a major supplier of agricultural products and raw materials means that the war has had significant global repercussions. The disruption of Ukrainian exports has led to shortages and increased prices for key commodities worldwide. Countries that relied heavily on Ukrainian wheat, for instance, have had to scramble to find alternative suppliers, affecting labor markets in those producing nations as they ramp up production to meet new demands.

This shift underscores the interconnectedness of global supply chains and how geopolitical events in one region can have cascading effects worldwide. Companies that were dependent on stable operations in Ukraine have had to adapt quickly, either by relocating their activities or by adjusting their supply chains to source materials from other regions. This need for agility emphasizes the importance of having flexible supply chain strategies that can withstand geopolitical disruptions.

The response of multinational corporations to the Ukraine war has further highlighted the interconnected nature of the global economy. Businesses with operations in Ukraine or those relying on Ukrainian suppliers have had to quickly adapt to the new reality. Some have relocated their production facilities to neighboring countries, while others have sought to diversify their supply chains to mitigate risks. This rapid adaptation has had a significant impact on labor markets, creating new job opportunities in some regions while leading to job losses in others.

Amid the conflict, technology has played a crucial role in maintaining business continuity. Companies have increasingly relied on digital communication tools and cloud-based platforms to coordinate their dispersed workforces. Remote work has become a vital component in managing the crisis, allowing employees to continue their tasks from safer locations. This shift reinforces the trend of remote work and demonstrates how technological advancements enable businesses to navigate geopolitical disruptions more effectively.

The Ukraine war is a solid example of the need for resilience and flexibility in the global job market. It has demonstrated how geopolitical events can swiftly alter economic landscapes, requiring quick adjustments from both workers and businesses. As we move forward, the ability to adapt to such changes will be crucial for both individuals and organizations.

For workers, this means a greater emphasis on acquiring adaptable skills and being open to new job opportunities, even in different regions or industries. For businesses, it highlights the importance of developing robust contingency plans and fostering a culture of agility that can respond to sudden geopolitical shifts.

Emerging Technologies and Job Creation

The arrival of new technologies has always played a crucial role in shaping the job market, creating new opportunities while transforming existing ones. As we advance further into the 21st century, the pace of technological innovation is accelerating, bringing with it profound implications for job creation and economic development globally.

Technological advancements have historically driven economic growth and job creation by enabling new industries and transforming existing ones. From the Industrial Revolution, which mechanized production and created manufacturing jobs, to the Digital Revolution, which has spawned entire industries around information technology, the pattern is clear: technology changes the nature of work and creates new opportunities.

AI and Machine Learning

AI and machine learning are at the forefront of technological innovation, creating job opportunities in areas such as data science, AI research, and machine learning engineering. These roles involve developing algorithms, analyzing data, and implementing AI solutions across various industries.

AI-driven automation also creates jobs by improving efficiencies and enabling the development of new products and services. For instance, AI in healthcare is leading to the creation of roles focused on developing diagnostic tools, personalized treatment plans, and managing AI-driven health systems.

Robotics and Automation

Robotics is transforming industries such as manufacturing, logistics, and healthcare. Jobs related to designing, building, and maintaining robotic systems are in high demand. This includes roles like robotics engineers, technicians, and programmers.

Automation is also driving job growth in sectors where it complements human labor rather than replacing it. For example, collaborative robots, or cobots (see next paragraph), work alongside humans, enhancing productivity and safety in the workplace.

Cobots, or collaborative robots, are designed to work alongside humans in a shared workspace. Unlike traditional industrial robots that operate in isolation, cobots are equipped with advanced sensors and safety features that allow them to interact safely and efficiently with human workers. These robots are used in various industries to assist with tasks that are repetitive, dangerous, or require precision, enhancing productivity and reducing the risk of injury. Cobots are easy to program and can be quickly adapted to different tasks, making them a flexible and valuable addition to modern manufacturing and production environments.

Beyond manufacturing, cobots have vast potential in numerous other fields. In the construction industry, cobots can be leveraged for building infrastructure in hazardous environments or even in outer space. NASA and other space agencies are exploring the use of cobots for constructing space habitats, repairing satellites, and performing maintenance on space stations. These robots can handle the harsh conditions of space, such as extreme temperatures and radiation, reducing the risk to human astronauts.

In the medical field, cobots are revolutionizing healthcare by assisting in surgeries, providing precise movements that surpass human capabilities. They are used in delicate procedures, such as neurosurgery and ophthalmology, where accuracy is paramount. Cobots also help with rehabilitation, aiding patients with physical therapy through repetitive, precise movements that ensure proper recovery.

Furthermore, cobots are becoming integral in disaster response scenarios. They can be deployed in environments that are too dangerous for humans, such as sites affected by natural disasters, nuclear accidents, or hazardous material spills. Equipped with advanced sensors and AI, cobots can navigate these environments, perform critical tasks such as search and rescue, and provide real-time data to human responders, improving the efficiency and safety of emergency operations.

As cobot technology continues to advance, their applications will expand, offering new opportunities across various sectors. Their ability to work collaboratively with humans while performing complex and hazardous tasks makes them indispensable in shaping the future of work and enhancing human capabilities in ways previously unimaginable.

The advancement of cobot technology will not only transform existing industries but also create a plethora of new job opportunities, many of which may seem like science fiction today. As cobots become more integrated into various sectors, new roles will emerge to support, manage, and innovate this technology.

One such role is the **Cobot Systems Integrator**, a specialist responsible for designing and implementing cobot systems within different environments. These professionals will work closely with engineers, programmers, and end-users to ensure that cobots are seamlessly integrated into workflows, maximizing their efficiency and safety.

Another emerging role could be that of a **Space Construction Supervisor**. As cobots take on the hazardous task of building infrastructure in outer space, humans will still be needed to oversee these projects from both Earth and space. These supervisors will coordinate between mission control, astronauts, and cobots to ensure that space habitats and other structures are constructed accurately and safely.

The **Cobot Health Technician** will be crucial in the medical field, responsible for maintaining and calibrating surgical cobots to ensure they function perfectly during delicate procedures. These technicians will need to have expertise in both robotics and medical equipment, bridging the gap between technology and healthcare.

In disaster response, a **Rescue Cobot Coordinator** will be needed to deploy and manage cobots in emergency situations. This role will involve strategizing the best use of cobots for search and rescue operations, ensuring they navigate hazardous environments effectively while providing real-time data to human responders.

Additionally, as cobots become more sophisticated, the demand for **Cobot Behavior Programmers** will rise. These specialists will develop and refine the AI algorithms that govern cobot behavior, ensuring they can adapt to new tasks and environments autonomously. This role will require a deep understanding of machine learning, robotics, and human-cobot interaction.

Furthermore, the role of a **Cobot Ethics Officer** will become increasingly important. This position will involve developing ethical guidelines and policies for the deployment and use of cobots, ensuring that their integration into society respects human rights, privacy, and safety.

Lastly, **Cobot Innovation Managers** will spearhead the development of new applications for cobots, pushing the boundaries of what these machines can do. They will work in research and development, collaborating with various industries to identify new opportunities and create cutting-edge solutions that leverage cobot technology.

As cobot technology continues to evolve, it will not only enhance human capabilities but also open up a world of new and exciting career paths, transforming the job market in ways we are just beginning to imagine.

Renewable Energy and Sustainability Technologies

The global shift toward sustainable energy sources is creating a surge in jobs related to renewable energy technologies. Positions in solar and wind energy production, energy storage, and sustainable construction are expanding rapidly. These roles are at the forefront of the green revolution, driving the transition to cleaner and more efficient energy systems. In addition to these traditional roles, the renewable energy sector is also giving rise to a host of futuristic and exciting job opportunities.

One such role is the **Renewable Energy Systems Architect**, who designs and integrates complex renewable energy systems, ensuring optimal performance and efficiency. These architects will work on large-scale projects, from city-wide smart grids to off-grid renewable energy solutions for remote areas. They will be responsible for creating sustainable energy infrastructures that are resilient, scalable, and capable of meeting the growing energy demands of the future.

Another emerging role is the **Energy Storage Specialist**. As renewable energy production increases, so does the need for efficient energy storage solutions. These specialists will develop and manage advanced storage technologies such as high-capacity batteries, hydrogen fuel cells, and thermal storage systems. Their work will ensure that energy produced from renewable sources is stored effectively and can be dispatched when needed, stabilizing the grid and enhancing energy reliability.

In the construction industry, **Sustainable Construction Managers** will lead the way in developing eco-friendly buildings and infrastructure. These managers will oversee projects that utilize sustainable materials, energy-efficient designs, and green building practices. Their goal will be to minimize the environmental impact of construction activities while maximizing the sustainability of the built environment.

Environmental monitoring is another area ripe for innovation. **Environmental Data Scientists** will analyze vast amounts of data collected from sensors, satellites, and drones to monitor ecosystems and track environmental changes. Their insights will be crucial for conservation efforts, helping to protect biodiversity and manage natural resources sustainably. These scientists will develop predictive models to forecast environmental trends and inform policy decisions, playing a critical role in preserving our planet's health.

The agricultural sector will also see transformative changes with the rise of **Sustainable Agriculture Technologists**. These professionals will develop and implement advanced farming techniques that reduce resource use and environmental impact. They will work on precision agriculture technologies, such as drones and AI-driven analytics, to optimize crop yields and manage soil health. Additionally, they will explore innovative practices like vertical farming and agroforestry to create more sustainable and resilient food systems.

As the renewable energy sector continues to grow, the need for **Green Finance Advisors** will become increasingly important. These advisors will specialize in financing sustainable projects, helping companies and governments secure funding for renewable energy initiatives. They will navigate the complexities of green finance, ensuring that investments are directed toward projects that deliver both environmental and economic benefits.

Lastly, the role of **Climate Resilience Analysts** will be vital in assessing and mitigating the impacts of climate change on communities and infrastructure. These analysts will develop strategies to enhance resilience, from designing flood defenses to planning for extreme weather events. Their work will help societies adapt to the changing climate, protecting lives and livelihoods while promoting sustainable development.

Biotechnology and Healthcare Innovations

Advances in biotechnology and healthcare technology are opening up a myriad of new roles in fields such as genetic engineering, bioinformatics, and personalized medicine. These innovative jobs involve researching and developing cutting-edge treatments, conducting clinical trials, and managing biotechnological applications. For instance, genetic engineers work on modifying the genetic makeup of organisms to develop new therapies for diseases, while bioinformaticians analyze complex biological data to advance our understanding of health and disease mechanisms.

As we delve deeper into personalized medicine, roles such as **Genetic Counselors** will become increasingly important. These professionals will interpret genetic tests and provide personalized healthcare advice to patients based on their genetic profiles. **Clinical Bioinformatics Specialists** will also be crucial, leveraging big data analytics to develop targeted treatments and improve patient outcomes.

The integration of technology in healthcare, such as telemedicine and health informatics, is leading to job growth in managing digital health platforms and ensuring data security and patient privacy. **Telehealth Coordinators** will manage virtual care systems, ensuring seamless communication between patients and healthcare providers. They will also be responsible for integrating AI-driven diagnostic tools that can assist doctors in making accurate and timely decisions.

Moreover, the rise of health informatics is creating roles for **Health Data Analysts** who will manage and interpret vast amounts of health data to optimize patient care and operational efficiency in healthcare settings. These analysts will play a key role in developing predictive models that can identify disease outbreaks and patient health trends.

In addition, advancements in biotechnology will spur the creation of jobs like **Biofabrication Engineers**, who will design and construct biological tissues and organs using 3D printing technology. This revolutionary approach could lead to breakthroughs in regenerative medicine, providing solutions for organ shortages and complex tissue repairs.

Another futuristic role could be that of a **Neurotechnology Specialist**. As we understand more about the brain and develop technologies that can interface with it, specialists will be needed to create and maintain neural prosthetics and brain-computer interfaces, offering new treatments for neurological disorders and enhancing cognitive abilities.

The advent of wearable health tech and implantable devices will also necessitate the need for **Biomedical Device Designers**. These professionals will create advanced health monitoring devices that provide real-time data to patients and doctors, enabling proactive healthcare management and personalized treatment plans.

In the area of genetic engineering, **CRISPR Technicians** will become pivotal. CRISPR, which stands for Clustered Regularly Interspaced Short Palindromic Repeats, is a revolutionary technology that allows scientists to edit genes with unprecedented precision. By using CRISPR, these specialists can make specific changes to the DNA sequence, potentially curing genetic disorders and enhancing human capabilities. The ability to edit genes with such accuracy opens up possibilities for treating conditions that were previously considered incurable. However, this powerful technology also raises significant ethical questions. As a result, there will be a growing demand for **Bioethics Advisors** who will navigate the moral and societal implications of genetic editing, ensuring that advancements are made responsibly and ethically.

As healthcare continues to evolve with technological integration, we will see the emergence of **AI Healthcare Trainers**. These experts will develop and refine AI algorithms that assist in diagnostics, treatment planning, and patient care, ensuring that AI systems are accurate, unbiased, and effective.

E-Commerce and Job Creation

Online Retail and Marketplace Jobs

E-commerce platforms like Amazon, Alibaba, and Shopify have transformed retail, creating a plethora of jobs in logistics, warehousing, customer service, and digital marketing. These roles support the vast infrastructure required to manage online sales, order fulfillment, and customer relations.

The gig economy, facilitated by platforms like Uber, Lyft, and TaskRabbit, has also expanded, providing flexible job opportunities for individuals seeking non-traditional work arrangements.

Digital Marketing and Content Creation

The growth of e-commerce has driven demand for digital marketing professionals, including search engine optimization specialists, social media managers, and content creators. These roles are essential for businesses to reach and engage online consumers.

Content creation has become a significant industry, with individuals and small businesses creating videos, blogs, and other media to attract and retain customers. Platforms like YouTube, Instagram, and TikTok have made it possible for content creators to monetize their work and build careers.

Digital Platforms and the Gig Economy

Freelancing and Remote Work Opportunities

Digital platforms such as Upwork, Fiverr, and Freelancer.com have enabled a global freelancing market, connecting skilled workers with clients across the world. This has democratized job opportunities, allowing individuals to work on projects that match their skills and interests, regardless of location.

Remote work technologies, such as Zoom, Slack, and Microsoft Teams, have facilitated the rise of remote job opportunities, allowing employees to work from anywhere and increasing job flexibility.

Specialized Skill Platforms

Platforms that focus on specific skill sets, like Toptal for tech talent or 99designs for graphic designers, have created niche markets where highly skilled professionals can find job opportunities tailored to their expertise.

These platforms have also enabled companies to access a broader talent pool, ensuring that they can find the best candidates for specialized roles.

Cloud services, offered by giants like Amazon Web Services (AWS) and Microsoft Azure, have been transformative in enabling people to create startups and develop applications with global impact. These platforms provide scalable, cost-effective infrastructure that allows entrepreneurs and developers to focus on innovation without the heavy upfront costs traditionally associated with building and maintaining physical servers.

These cloud services democratize access to powerful computing resources, making it possible for individuals and small teams to launch startups with minimal initial investment. By offering a range of services, including computing power, storage, databases, machine learning, and analytics, cloud platforms lower the barriers to entry for startups. Entrepreneurs can prototype, develop, and deploy applications quickly, scaling their operations as demand grows. One of the key advantages of cloud services is their scalability. Startups can begin with a small amount of resources and seamlessly scale up as their user base expands. This flexibility is crucial for managing growth without overcommitting resources or facing downtime. Additionally, cloud services often include integrated tools for continuous integration and continuous deployment (CI/CD), which streamline the development process and enhance productivity.

The impact of cloud services on job creation extends beyond the startups themselves. By enabling global reach and remote collaboration, cloud platforms create additional job opportunities in different geographies. Developers, IT professionals, digital marketers, and customer support teams can work from anywhere, supporting the operations of cloud-enabled startups. Cloud services also foster an ecosystem of ancillary businesses and services. Managed service providers, consulting firms, and training institutions emerge to support companies using cloud platforms, further expanding job opportunities. Additionally, as startups grow and scale, they contribute to local economies by hiring employees, renting office spaces, and investing in community development.

A prime example of a startup leveraging cloud services to achieve global impact is Slack. Slack, a collaboration and communication platform, started as an internal tool for a gaming company and quickly grew into a globally recognized enterprise software provider. Utilizing AWS for its infrastructure, Slack was able to scale rapidly to meet the needs of millions of users worldwide. By building on AWS, Slack could focus on developing its core product without worrying about the complexities of managing servers and infrastructure. AWS provided the necessary scalability and reliability, allowing Slack to handle massive amounts of data and user interactions seamlessly. As Slack grew, it created a multitude of jobs, not only within its own company but also through an ecosystem of developers building integrations and bots for the Slack platform. Moreover, Slack's global reach enabled it to employ a diverse, distributed workforce, hiring talent from various regions to support its operations. This approach demonstrated how cloud services could facilitate a globally connected, innovative workforce, contributing to job creation and economic growth across different geographies.

Cloud services from providers like Amazon and Microsoft have revolutionized the way startups are built and operated, enabling entrepreneurs to develop and deploy applications with global impact. By offering scalable, flexible, and cost-effective solutions, these platforms reduce the barriers to entry for innovation and support rapid growth. This shift drives the success of individual startups and on top generates job opportunities across the globe, illustrating the profound influence of cloud technology on the modern economy.

Shifts in Global Economic Power and Employment

As we navigate the complex landscape of the global economy, it is essential to understand how shifts in economic power are influencing employment and redefining the nature of jobs. These changes are driven by various factors, including technological advancements, economic policies, and the evolving capabilities of developing nations. By examining these shifts, we can gain insights into the future of work and the dynamic interplay between different regions.

The globalization of labor markets has led to a significant redistribution of jobs. In developed countries like the United States and those within Europe, there has been a noticeable shift in the types of jobs available. Repetitive tasks in factories and call centers, which once provided steady employment for many, have increasingly been outsourced to developing countries. This shift is driven by the ability of these countries to adopt relevant technologies and train their workforce to handle these tasks at a lower cost. For instance, countries like India and the Philippines have become global hubs for call centers and back-office operations, providing job opportunities for millions of people with lower to mid-level skills.

This transition has had profound effects on employment patterns in developed countries. As low-skill, repetitive jobs moved offshore, workers in Europe and the United States found themselves needing to adapt. The necessity to elevate their skills became apparent, pushing many toward higher education and vocational training programs aimed at more advanced, specialized roles. This shift has been critical in transforming the workforce, driving innovation, and creating new job categories that require advanced technical skills, creativity, and problem-solving capabilities.

In developing countries, the influx of outsourced jobs has spurred economic growth and industrialization. By embracing new technologies and improving educational infrastructure, these countries have been able to offer employment opportunities to a large segment of their population, thereby lifting many out of poverty. The growth of industries in these regions has created jobs and at the same time required the development of new skill sets, fostering a more capable and versatile workforce.

This pattern is not entirely new; it echoes the transformations seen during the Industrial Revolution. During that period, countries like the UK, Germany, and the Nordic nations were at the forefront of industrial development, offering advanced job opportunities to their populations. These jobs attracted workers from rural areas and other regions, driving urbanization and economic development. The migration of labor to burgeoning industrial centers was a key factor in the economic expansion and societal changes of the time.

Today, we observe a similar phenomenon on a global scale. Workers migrate not only within countries but also across borders, seeking better job opportunities and higher incomes. This mobility is facilitated by advancements in transportation and communication technologies, making it easier for people to relocate for work. Additionally, the rise of remote work, accelerated by the COVID-19 pandemic, has further blurred geographical boundaries, allowing individuals to work for companies based in different parts of the world without the need to physically relocate.

As developing countries continue to industrialize and integrate into the global economy, the nature of work will keep evolving. Jobs that require routine manual labor are likely to remain concentrated in regions where labor costs are lower. Meanwhile, developed countries will increasingly focus on high-skill, knowledge-based jobs that drive innovation and economic growth. This bifurcation of job types mandates continuous adaptation and skill development from workers in both developed and developing nations.

Furthermore, the rapid pace of technological change means that the skills required for many jobs today may become obsolete tomorrow. Continuous learning and flexibility will be key for workers to stay relevant in the job market. Governments and educational institutions will play a crucial role in providing the necessary training and resources to help the workforce adapt to these changes.

The shifting economic power across the globe is fundamentally altering the landscape of employment. Developing countries are becoming the new industrial hubs, absorbing jobs that involve repetitive tasks, while developed nations are transitioning toward advanced, knowledge-based economies. This dynamic creates both challenges and opportunities, requiring a global workforce that is adaptable, skilled, and ready to meet the demands of an ever-changing job market. By understanding these trends and preparing for their implications, we can better prepare for the future of work and ensure that the benefits of economic progress are broadly shared.

Geopolitical Trends and Labor Markets

Geopolitical trends have always played a critical role in shaping global employment and job stability. The interplay between nations, driven by political, economic, and social factors, often leads to shifts that profoundly impact labor markets. Understanding these impacts requires a close examination of how geopolitical events influence economic policies, trade relationships, and, consequently, job opportunities and security.

One of the most significant ways geopolitical events impact global employment is through changes in trade policies. Trade wars, for instance, can create substantial volatility in job markets. When countries impose tariffs or sanctions on each other, it disrupts the flow of goods and services, leading to decreased production, higher costs for consumers and businesses, and ultimately, job losses. The recent trade tensions between the United States and China serve as a prime example.

The imposition of tariffs on a wide range of products affected companies relying on imported goods and led to retaliatory measures, creating uncertainty and instability in various sectors such as manufacturing, agriculture, and technology. Companies facing increased costs might cut back on investments, freeze hiring, or even lay off workers to manage their expenses.

There are historical examples where trade wars or trade policies have led to the creation of new types of jobs in specific regions or countries. One notable example is the Smoot-Hawley Tariff Act of 1930. This act significantly raised U.S. tariffs on imported goods, aiming to protect American businesses and farmers from foreign competition. In response to the tariffs, many countries retaliated with tariffs of their own, leading to a significant decrease in international trade. This forced American businesses to become more self-reliant and look for ways to produce goods domestically that were previously imported.

One of the sectors that saw a significant shift was the American synthetic rubber industry. Before the tariffs, the U.S. heavily relied on natural rubber imports from Southeast Asia. The trade barriers, along with the disruptions caused by World War II, led to shortages of natural rubber, which was critical for various industries, particularly the automotive and military sectors. To address this shortage, the U.S. government and private companies invested heavily in research and development to create synthetic rubber. This initiative was part of a broader effort called the Synthetic Rubber Program, which brought together scientists, engineers, and workers from various backgrounds to develop and scale up synthetic rubber production. The program led to significant advancements in polymer chemistry and the creation of a robust synthetic rubber industry in the United States.

As a result, new types of jobs emerged in chemical engineering, polymer science, and industrial production. Factories were built, and a skilled workforce was developed to manufacture synthetic rubber and its derivatives. These advancements not only met domestic needs but also positioned the U.S. as a leader in synthetic materials, with applications extending beyond rubber to plastics and other synthetic products.

Another example can be found in the tech industry, particularly during the Cold War era. The technological and geopolitical competition between the United States and the Soviet Union led to significant government investment in research and development, particularly in fields like aerospace, computing, and telecommunications. These investments were partially a response to trade restrictions and the need for technological superiority. The result was the creation of entirely new industries and job types, including roles in computer science, software development, and aerospace engineering, which have continued to evolve and expand into the modern tech industry.

These examples illustrate how trade wars and geopolitical tensions can drive innovation and lead to the creation of new types of jobs. By forcing regions or countries to become more self-reliant and invest in new technologies and industries, trade policies can inadvertently foster job creation and economic diversification. For instance, the trade tensions between the United States and China have led to significant shifts in global supply chains. Companies facing higher tariffs have been compelled to relocate their production facilities to other countries to avoid additional costs.

This shift has created new manufacturing jobs in countries like Vietnam, Mexico, and India, as these nations have become attractive alternatives for companies looking to diversify their supply chains.

Trade wars can also spur domestic innovation and job creation in certain sectors. When access to foreign goods is restricted, countries may invest in developing their own industries to reduce dependency on imports. For example, the United States' tariffs on Chinese technology products have accelerated the growth of the domestic semiconductor industry. Companies have increased investments in research and development to enhance their technological capabilities and ensure a stable supply of critical components. This shift has resulted in new jobs in high-tech manufacturing, engineering, and research roles within the United States.

Regional conflicts also have significant implications for labor markets. Conflicts can devastate local economies, displacing millions of people and disrupting businesses. The ongoing conflict in Syria, for example, has led to a massive refugee crisis, with millions fleeing to neighboring countries and beyond. These displaced individuals often struggle to find stable employment, contributing to economic strain in host countries. At the same time, countries directly involved in conflicts face destruction of infrastructure, loss of human capital, and long-term economic instability, making job recovery a monumental challenge.

Geopolitical instability extends to global supply chains. Modern supply chains are intricate and highly interconnected, relying on stable political and economic environments to function smoothly. Disruptions can cause significant delays and increase costs, as companies scramble to find alternative sources or routes for their goods. This can lead to job losses in industries dependent on just-in-time production and global logistics, such as automotive manufacturing and electronics.

The ongoing conflict in Ukraine, for example, has impacted the supply of essential commodities like wheat and natural gas. European countries, heavily reliant on these imports, have had to seek alternative sources, leading to changes in agricultural production and energy sectors. This shift has created new job opportunities in regions that can provide these resources, while also driving innovation in renewable energy and sustainable agricultural practices to reduce future dependency on geopolitical hotspots.

Moreover, geopolitical events often prompt shifts in foreign direct investment (FDI). Investors seek stability and predictability, and heightened geopolitical risks can deter investment in affected regions. Countries experiencing political unrest or conflict may see a decline in FDI, which is crucial for economic development and job creation. Conversely, countries perceived as safe havens might attract more investment, boosting their economies and creating new job opportunities.

Geopolitical alliances and economic blocs, such as the European Union, also influence labor markets by shaping trade policies and labor mobility. The European Union's single market allows for the free movement of goods, services, capital, and labor across member states, facilitating job creation and economic growth. However, political events like Brexit have highlighted the fragility of these arrangements. The UK's departure from the EU has introduced uncertainties for businesses and workers, leading to potential labor shortages in key sectors such as healthcare and agriculture, which have traditionally relied on migrant labor from other EU countries.

Environmental policies driven by international agreements can lead to significant shifts in labor markets. The global push towards sustainability, exemplified by the Paris Agreement, has led to the creation of green jobs in renewable energy, energy efficiency, and environmental conservation. Countries committed to reducing carbon emissions are investing in solar and wind power projects, energy-efficient building technologies, and sustainable transportation systems. These investments generate new employment opportunities in engineering, construction, maintenance, and environmental sciences, while also necessitating the retraining of workers from traditional fossil fuel industries.

The rise of remote work, accelerated by the COVID-19 pandemic, is another geopolitical trend impacting labor markets. Remote work has enabled companies to tap into a global talent pool, allowing employees to work from anywhere in the world. This trend has led to increased job opportunities in regions with lower living costs, as companies seek to optimize their workforce expenses. Additionally, remote work has driven demand for digital infrastructure and services, creating jobs in IT support, cybersecurity, and cloud computing.

Geopolitical trends are integral to understanding the dynamics of global labor markets. Trade wars, regional conflicts, shifting alliances, and environmental policies all play significant roles in shaping employment patterns and job stability. By analyzing these trends, we can anticipate the challenges and opportunities that lie ahead, ensuring that both workers and businesses are prepared to navigate an increasingly complex and interconnected global economy.

Transformation of Global Supply Chains and Employment

The transformation of global supply chains is poised to be one of the most dynamic areas of change in the future, driven by technological advancements and geopolitical shifts. These factors are reshaping the way supply chains operate and creating a plethora of new job opportunities that were previously unimaginable. As we look toward the future, it is essential to explore how these changes will impact supply chain jobs and what new roles may emerge.

Technological advancements, particularly in AI, robotics, and the IoT, are revolutionizing supply chain management.

These technological innovations are transforming traditional supply chain jobs and creating new roles that require a blend of technical and analytical skills. For instance, supply chain analysts will increasingly rely on AI and data analytics to make strategic decisions, while logistics coordinators will need to manage fleets of autonomous vehicles and drones. The integration of these technologies will also give rise to roles such as IoT specialists, who will be responsible for implementing and maintaining IoT devices throughout the supply chain.

Geopolitical shifts are also playing a significant role in the transformation of global supply chains. Trade tensions, such as those between the United States and China, as we mentioned in the book previously, are prompting companies to diversify their supply sources and reduce dependency on any single country. This shift is leading to the development of more resilient and flexible supply chain models, with a focus on regionalization and nearshoring. As companies establish new manufacturing and distribution hubs closer to their key markets, they will create job opportunities in these regions.

In the future, we can expect to see the emergence of **supply chain resilience managers**, whose primary role will be to assess and mitigate risks associated with geopolitical uncertainties. These professionals will need to develop strategies to ensure continuity of supply in the face of disruptions, such as trade wars, natural disasters, or political instability. Their expertise will be crucial in helping companies navigate the complex landscape of global trade and maintain a competitive edge.

Another exciting development in supply chain management is the increasing emphasis on sustainability. As environmental concerns become more pressing, companies are seeking ways to reduce their carbon footprint and adopt more sustainable practices. This shift is creating new job opportunities in areas such as sustainable sourcing, where professionals will be responsible for identifying and partnering with environmentally responsible suppliers. Additionally, roles such as **circular economy specialists** will focus on developing strategies to minimize waste and promote the reuse and recycling of materials throughout the supply chain.

Advancements in blockchain technology are also set to transform supply chain management by providing greater transparency and security. Blockchain can create immutable records of transactions, ensuring the authenticity and traceability of goods. This technology will give rise to new roles such as **blockchain supply chain analysts**, who will be responsible for implementing blockchain solutions and ensuring the integrity of supply chain data.

The rise of e-commerce is another factor driving changes in supply chain jobs. As online shopping continues to grow, the demand for efficient and responsive supply chains has never been higher. This trend is leading to the creation of roles such as **e-commerce logistics managers**, who will oversee the rapid fulfillment and delivery of online orders. These professionals will need to leverage advanced technologies and innovative strategies to meet the expectations of increasingly demanding consumers.

Looking further into the future, we can anticipate the development of entirely new job categories as supply chain management becomes more integrated with cutting-edge technologies. For example, augmented reality (AR) and virtual reality (VR) could revolutionize warehouse management and training. AR can provide real-time guidance to warehouse workers, enhancing their efficiency and accuracy, while VR can be used to simulate complex supply chain scenarios for training purposes. This will create demand for **AR/VR supply chain specialists** who can design and implement these immersive technologies.

As supply chains become more automated and data-driven, the importance of cybersecurity will also increase. Protecting sensitive supply chain data from cyber threats will be extremely necessary, leading to the emergence of specialized roles such as **supply chain cybersecurity analysts**. These professionals will be tasked with safeguarding the integrity of supply chain systems and ensuring that data remains secure throughout the entire process.

Remote Work and the Global Talent Pool

One topic I am especially passionate about and have expertise in is remote work and the global talent pool, driven not only by technology but also by freelancing platforms. As I covered extensively in my last book, *Leading the Unknown*, the world was already moving toward remote and hybrid work before the pandemic, thanks to technological advancements. The integration of freelancing talent from across the globe was becoming more prevalent, with businesses recognizing the need for a 24/7 operational capability that local resources alone couldn't provide. This diversification brings innovation and creativity, positioning companies more competitively in the global market.

The rise of remote work has had a significant impact on global job markets. In the past, companies were largely limited to hiring locally, which restricted their access to a broader market and stifled creativity. Now, with remote work technology, AI, and freelancing platforms, businesses are increasingly moving toward a global workforce. This shift is changing the dynamics of employment and altering the flow of money across borders. Previously, companies were confined to specific regions, requiring physical offices and daily commutes for employees. However, the need for traditional office spaces has diminished, and people can work effectively and securely from anywhere.

The impact of remote work on daily life is profound. The average commute for those working from home is now just a matter of seconds, significantly reducing the environmental footprint of daily travel. This shift contributes to sustainability efforts by decreasing traffic congestion and pollution, while also enhancing work-life balance. Employees can spend more time with their families and enjoy a better quality of life, as they are no longer bound by the constraints of commuting.

Technological advancements have made remote work more secure and productive. AI tools and cloud platforms enable workers to enhance their productivity and quality of outcomes. These technologies support secure remote work environments, ensuring that both companies and freelancers can operate efficiently and safely. The integration of AI into these platforms allows for better management of tasks, streamlined communication, and enhanced collaboration, leading to improved performance and innovation.

The benefits of remote work extend beyond individual productivity. Companies benefit from a more diverse and innovative workforce. By hiring talent from different regions and backgrounds, businesses can foster a more inclusive environment that encourages diverse perspectives and ideas. This diversity is crucial for driving creativity and innovation, which are key to maintaining a competitive edge in the global market.

Governments and companies must and will adapt to these changes by updating laws and regulations to support remote work and freelancing. Providing the necessary technologies and ensuring social benefits for remote workers are essential steps in facilitating this transition. Digital nomad visas and other policies that allow workers to live and work in different countries can help integrate global talent more seamlessly. These measures support economic growth and promote cultural exchange and collaboration across borders.

As we move forward, the interaction between cultures and the exchange of experiences will become even more important. The ability for people to work remotely from different parts of the world enhances their exposure to diverse viewpoints and practices. This cultural interchange can lead to greater empathy, understanding, and collaboration, fostering a more connected and harmonious global workforce.

The shift toward remote work and the increasing reliance on a global talent pool offer a multitude of opportunities for businesses. One of the most significant benefits is access to a broader range of skills and expertise. Companies are no longer limited by geographic boundaries when seeking the best talent for specific roles. This allows organizations to find highly specialized professionals who may be scarce in their local markets, thus enhancing the quality of work and driving innovation. For instance, a startup in San Francisco can hire a top-tier data scientist from India, a creative UX designer from Brazil, and an experienced project manager from Germany, all working together seamlessly thanks to remote work technologies. This diverse talent pool can lead to a more dynamic and innovative workforce, capable of tackling complex challenges with a variety of perspectives and solutions.

Another notable opportunity is the potential for cost savings. Labor costs can vary significantly across different regions, and hiring skilled professionals in countries where the cost of living is lower can result in substantial savings for companies. This approach allows businesses to optimize their budgets while still accessing high-quality talent. Additionally, the flexibility of remote work arrangements can lead to increased employee satisfaction and retention, as workers appreciate the ability to balance their professional and personal lives more effectively.

However, tapping into a global talent pool also presents several challenges. One of the primary challenges is managing a geographically dispersed team. Differences in time zones, cultural backgrounds, and communication styles can create obstacles in collaboration and workflow. Effective communication and project management tools are essential and exist to overcome these barriers and ensure that remote teams can work cohesively. Companies must invest in technology and processes that facilitate smooth communication and collaboration across different locations and time zones. This includes regular virtual meetings, clear and concise communication channels, and tools that support real-time collaboration.

Ensuring data security and compliance with international regulations is another significant challenge. Remote work often involves accessing sensitive company data from various locations, which can increase the risk of data breaches. Companies must implement robust cybersecurity measures to protect their information and ensure compliance with data protection laws in different jurisdictions. This may involve using secure communication tools, encrypting sensitive data, and providing regular cybersecurity training for employees to mitigate risks.

Cultural differences can also pose challenges in a global workforce. Different cultural norms and practices can lead to misunderstandings and miscommunications, which can affect team dynamics and productivity. Companies need to foster an inclusive culture that respects and values diversity. This involves providing cultural competency training for employees, promoting open and respectful communication, and creating opportunities for team members to learn about each other's backgrounds and perspectives.

Another challenge remote workers may face is isolation and a lack of connection with their teams. Building a strong company culture and maintaining employee engagement can be more challenging in a remote work environment. Companies need to invest in virtual team-building activities, regular check-ins, and creating opportunities for remote employees to feel connected and valued. This might include virtual social events, mentorship programs, and regular feedback sessions to ensure that remote workers feel integrated and supported.

Tapping into a global talent pool offers tremendous opportunities for businesses, including access to a broader range of skills, potential cost savings, and increased flexibility. However, it also presents challenges such as managing a dispersed team, ensuring data security, navigating cultural differences, and maintaining employee engagement. By addressing these challenges proactively, companies can leverage the benefits of a global workforce to drive innovation, productivity, and growth in an increasingly interconnected world.

Economic Inequality and Workforce Policies

Economic inequality has become a pressing issue both within and between countries, with profound implications for workers and the broader economy. The disparity in income and wealth distribution has been widening for decades, driven by various factors including globalization, technological advancements, and differing national policies. This inequality affects individuals' quality of life and hampers economic growth and social cohesion.

According to the World Inequality Report 2022[3], the top 1% of earners captured 20.1% of global income in 2021, while the bottom 50% earned only 8.5%. This stark disparity is even more pronounced when considering wealth distribution, with the top 1% owning 43.4% of global wealth compared to the bottom 50% holding just 2.0%. Such levels of inequality can lead to significant social and economic challenges, including reduced social mobility, increased poverty rates, and heightened social tensions.

Within countries, economic inequality often manifests in the form of wage gaps and unequal access to opportunities. In the United States, for example, the median wage has stagnated over the past few decades despite rising productivity. The Economic Policy Institute report[4] states that between 1979 and 2020, productivity grew by 61.8%, while the median hourly compensation increased by only 17.5%. This disconnect between productivity and wage growth has contributed to rising income inequality and a shrinking middle class.

Technological advancements, while driving economic growth and innovation, have also contributed to economic inequality. Automation and AI are displacing low-skill jobs while creating high-skill positions that require advanced education and training. This shift disproportionately benefits those with access to higher education and technical skills, leaving behind workers in traditional industries. According to a study by McKinsey Global

Institute[5], up to 800 million workers worldwide could be displaced by automation by 2030, exacerbating income disparities unless proactive measures are taken.

Economic inequality between countries is also a significant issue. Developing nations often struggle with lower income levels, limited access to quality education and healthcare, and fewer economic opportunities. The International Labor Organization (ILO)[6] estimates that over 630 million workers worldwide lived in extreme or moderate poverty in 2019, with the majority residing in developing countries. These disparities can stifle global economic growth and contribute to migration pressures as individuals seek better opportunities abroad.

To address these growing inequalities and promote inclusive job growth, comprehensive policy responses are needed. These policies must focus on reducing disparities in income and wealth, ensuring equal access to education and training, and supporting vulnerable populations.

One effective policy response is the implementation of progressive taxation. By taxing higher incomes and wealth at greater rates, governments can redistribute resources and fund social programs that benefit lower-income individuals. Countries like Sweden and Denmark have successfully used progressive taxation to reduce income inequality and provide robust social safety nets. These measures have contributed to higher levels of social mobility and overall economic stability.

Investing in education and training is another crucial policy response. Ensuring that all individuals have access to quality education and lifelong learning opportunities can help bridge the skills gap and enable workers to adapt to changing job markets. Countries like Germany and Denmark have strong vocational training systems that prepare workers for high-skill jobs in various industries. Expanding such programs globally can enhance workforce resilience and reduce inequality.

Implementing and enforcing labor standards is also essential. Policies that promote fair wages, safe working conditions, and the right to organize can protect workers' rights and improve their economic security. The International Labor Organization's Decent Work Agenda emphasizes the importance of such standards in achieving social justice and inclusive growth. By adopting and enforcing these standards, countries can ensure that economic growth benefits all workers, not just the privileged few.

Social safety nets, such as unemployment insurance, healthcare, and pensions, are critical for supporting workers during economic transitions. These programs provide a buffer against economic shocks and help individuals maintain their living standards while they seek new employment opportunities. Countries like Canada and the Netherlands have comprehensive social safety nets that support workers through job losses and retraining efforts, promoting economic stability and inclusivity.

Finally, fostering inclusive economic growth requires international cooperation and support for developing countries. Global institutions like the World Bank and the International Monetary Fund (IMF) can play a crucial role in providing financial assistance and technical expertise to help developing nations build resilient economies. Additionally, trade policies that promote fair and equitable access to markets can support sustainable development and reduce global inequality.

Productivity Versus Income In The Future Of Work

In the future of work, productivity will soar to unprecedented heights, propelled by the seamless integration of AI into everyday tasks. Picture a world where AI-powered assistants and collaborative robots (cobots) are ubiquitous, enhancing human capabilities rather than replacing them. In this envisioned future, workers will experience a dynamic shift in how they approach their roles, leading to substantial increases in both productivity and income.

In this future, AI will automate routine tasks, freeing up human workers to focus on creative, strategic, and complex problem-solving activities. For instance, AI will handle data entry, scheduling, and customer service inquiries with impeccable efficiency, allowing employees to dedicate their time to innovation and value creation. This shift will both improve productivity and position workers to demand higher wages for their enhanced contributions.

As productivity skyrockets, companies will recognize the importance of fairly distributing the economic benefits. Performance-based compensation models will become the norm, directly linking individual and team outputs to financial rewards. Employees will receive instant feedback on their performance through advanced analytics, enabling them to continuously improve and see the immediate impact of their efforts on their income. This transparent and real-time approach to performance management will ensure that productivity gains translate directly into higher earnings.

In this future landscape, the gig economy will flourish with AI-driven platforms that match freelancers with projects tailored to their skills and preferences. These platforms will use sophisticated algorithms to ensure that gig workers are compensated fairly based on the complexity and value of their contributions. As a result, gig workers will enjoy more stable and predictable incomes, with their earnings reflecting the true value of their productivity.

Moreover, AI will play a crucial role in continuous learning and skill development. Personalized learning platforms, powered by AI, will provide employees with tailored training programs, helping them stay ahead of industry trends and technological advancements. This ongoing education will enable workers to upskill and reskill, making them more valuable to their employers and justifying higher salaries. The investment in human capital will pay off as companies reap the benefits of a highly skilled and adaptable workforce.

The future workplace will also see a rise in profit-sharing and employee stock ownership plans (ESOPs). As companies achieve higher productivity through AI, they will implement these programs to ensure that employees share in the financial success. Workers will become partial owners of the companies they contribute to, aligning their interests with those of the business. This sense of ownership will drive motivation and loyalty, further boosting productivity and income.

Government policies will evolve to support this new paradigm. Progressive taxation and incentives for companies that invest in their workforce will create a more equitable distribution of wealth. Policies will encourage fair compensation practices and provide safety nets for gig workers, ensuring that the benefits of increased productivity are shared broadly across society. Labor laws will be updated to protect the rights of workers in an AI-driven economy, promoting fair wages and job security.

In the future, the collaborative nature of AI and human work will foster a culture of innovation and continuous improvement. AI will analyze vast amounts of data to identify trends, opportunities, and efficiencies that humans might overlook. Employees will leverage these insights to make informed decisions, drive strategic initiatives, and develop new products and services. The resulting increase in productivity will lead to higher revenues and profits, which companies will reinvest in their workforce, creating a virtuous cycle of growth and prosperity.

Ultimately, in this future of work, the synergy between AI and human labor will transform industries and redefine the concept of productivity. Workers will enjoy more fulfilling and financially rewarding careers, as they harness the power of AI to achieve greater heights of efficiency and creativity. This future will be characterized by a harmonious balance between technological advancement and human potential, where productivity gains translate into tangible economic benefits for all.

In the future of work, I believe we will witness a profound transformation driven by technology, policy innovation, and a heightened emphasis on inclusivity. This future will be characterized by several key developments that will shape the global economy and redefine the nature of work.

In this new era, the concept of work will expand beyond traditional employment models. The rise of the gig economy and freelancing platforms will continue, allowing individuals to offer their skills and expertise on a project-by-project basis. This flexibility will enable workers to balance their professional and personal lives more effectively, leading to higher job satisfaction and overall well-being. Furthermore, the global talent pool will become even more accessible, allowing companies to tap into diverse skill sets from around the world.

Economic inequality will be addressed through innovative policies that promote equitable growth and opportunity. Governments will implement progressive taxation systems and invest heavily in education and training to ensure that all individuals have the chance to succeed in the new economy. Lifelong learning will become the norm, with continuous education and skill development integrated into the fabric of society. This commitment to education will ensure that workers are equipped with the skills needed to thrive in an ever-changing job market.

Social safety nets will evolve to provide more comprehensive support for workers. Universal basic income (UBI) or similar programs could be introduced to guarantee a minimum standard of living, regardless of employment status. This security will allow individuals to take risks, pursue entrepreneurial endeavors, and invest in their personal and professional growth without the fear of financial instability. Enhanced healthcare and retirement benefits will also ensure that workers can enjoy a high quality of life throughout their careers and into retirement.

The future of work will also see a greater emphasis on sustainability and corporate social responsibility. Businesses will prioritize environmentally friendly practices and ethical supply chains, driven by both regulatory requirements and consumer demand. Green jobs in renewable energy, conservation, and sustainable agriculture will proliferate, contributing to a more sustainable global economy. This focus on sustainability will not only protect the planet but also create new economic opportunities and drive long-term growth.

Workplaces themselves will undergo significant changes, becoming more inclusive and supportive of diverse work arrangements. Remote and hybrid work models will become the norm, supported by advanced digital infrastructure and collaboration tools. Companies will invest in creating inclusive work environments that accommodate the needs of all employees, including those with disabilities or caregiving responsibilities. This inclusive approach will enhance employee engagement, retention, and productivity.

In the future of work, I believe that the convergence of technology, policy innovation, and a commitment to inclusivity will drive a more equitable and prosperous global economy. This transformation will enable individuals to reach their full potential, businesses to innovate and grow, and societies to thrive in an interconnected and sustainable world. By embracing these changes and preparing for the future, we can create a world where work is not only a means of economic survival but also a source of personal fulfillment and societal progress.

Generational Voices: Millennial and Gen Z Influences on Work Culture

To understand the future of work, we need to analyze in depth what drives Millennials and Gen Z, as they are integral to today's workforce and will be pivotal in shaping the work practices and culture of the future. Millennials, typically defined as those born between 1981 and 1996, are now between 28 and 43 years old. They have grown up during a period of rapid technological change, globalization, and economic disruption, which has significantly influenced their values, expectations, and behaviors in the workplace.

Generation Z, the cohort following Millennials, encompasses those born between 1997 and 2012, making them between 12 and 27 years old today. As digital natives, Gen Z has been immersed in technology from a young age, with the internet, social media, and mobile devices playing a central role in their daily lives. This constant connectivity has shaped their communication styles, learning preferences, and career aspirations.

Both generations are characterized by their adaptability, tech-savviness, and desire for meaningful work. They prioritize work-life balance, flexibility, and opportunities for growth and development. Millennials, having experienced economic instability during the Great Recession of 2008, value job security and are more likely to seek employers that offer stability and clear career progression. Gen Z, on the other hand, tends to be more entrepreneurial, with a significant portion expressing interest in starting their businesses or engaging in freelance work.

A survey by Deloitte[7] in 2021 highlighted that 44% of Millennials and 49% of Gen Z would consider leaving their jobs within two years if they feel their employers do not align with their values or do not provide adequate career advancement opportunities. This statistic underscores the importance of understanding and addressing the unique needs and expectations of these generations to retain top talent and foster a positive work culture.

In addition to valuing flexibility and work-life balance, Millennials and Gen Z are deeply concerned about social and environmental issues. They prefer to work for organizations that demonstrate a commitment to corporate social responsibility, sustainability, and ethical practices. This trend is pushing companies to adopt more transparent and socially responsible business practices to attract and retain these workers.

Moreover, the emphasis on diversity and inclusion is stronger among these younger generations. They seek workplaces that are inclusive and diverse, not just in terms of gender and ethnicity, but also in terms of thought, background, and experience.

As we delve deeper into the influences of Millennials and Gen Z on work culture, it becomes clear that these generations are not just participants in the workforce but are active agents of change. I constantly notice this in my day-to day interactions with this group in the world-wide program I am running in Microsoft. Their preferences and values are reshaping organizational structures, workplace policies, and leadership styles including mine. By understanding and adapting to these generational drivers, businesses can better navigate the evolving landscape of work and build a more engaged, productive, and future-ready workforce.

As we look into the future of work, Millennials and Gen Z are poised to drive unprecedented changes in how businesses operate, the nature of work itself, and the overall workplace culture. Their distinct values, experiences, and expectations will redefine what it means to work and thrive in a professional environment. These two generations will have a multiplier effect on the future of work, setting the stage for transformative shifts that will unfold over the coming decades.

Millennials and Gen Z value flexibility in their work arrangements, seeking opportunities that allow them to balance their professional and personal lives more effectively. This demand for flexibility has already accelerated the adoption of remote and hybrid work models. In the future, we can expect more companies to offer flexible schedules, remote work options, and even shorter workweeks to attract and retain top talent. This shift will also influence how office spaces are designed, with a focus on creating collaborative environments that cater to both in-person and remote workers.

A notable trend is the unprecedented shrinking of traditional office spaces. Companies are increasingly opting for smaller, more flexible office spaces as they embrace remote and hybrid work models. This downsizing has led to a surplus of commercial real estate, prompting many property owners to convert office buildings into residential properties. For instance, in cities like

New York and San Francisco, developers are transforming unused office spaces into apartments and condos, catering to the growing demand for urban housing.

In tandem with the reduction of traditional office spaces, coworking spaces are experiencing a remarkable proliferation. These shared work environments offer flexible, short-term leases and a variety of amenities that cater to the needs of remote and freelance workers. According to a report by Coworking Resources[8], the number of coworking spaces worldwide is expected to reach approximately 40,000 by 2024, up from around 26,000 in 2020. This growth reflects the rising demand for flexible workspaces that provide a sense of community and collaboration, which are often lacking in remote work setups.

Coworking spaces are not only popular among freelancers and startups but are also being adopted by larger corporations looking to provide their employees with flexible work options. Companies such as IBM, Microsoft, and Spotify have incorporated coworking spaces into their real estate strategies, allowing their employees to work from convenient locations while still accessing the resources and networking opportunities these spaces offer.

The design of these coworking spaces is tailored to foster collaboration and innovation. They often feature open-plan layouts, communal areas, and amenities like high-speed internet, meeting rooms, and recreational facilities. This environment contrasts sharply with the traditional, segmented office layout and is more conducive to the dynamic work styles favored by Millennials and Gen Z.

In addition to coworking spaces, the trend toward more flexible office environments is leading to the development of "hub-and-spoke" models, where companies maintain a central headquarter (the hub) and multiple smaller satellite offices (the spokes) closer to where employees live. This model reduces commute times and provides employees with the flexibility to choose where they work, enhancing their work-life balance.

As these trends continue to unfold, the transformation of office spaces will play a crucial role in shaping the future of work. The shift toward flexibility, driven by the preferences of Millennials and Gen Z, is leading to more adaptive and innovative workplace solutions. These changes are redefining where and how we work and are fostering a more sustainable and balanced approach to professional life. The evolution of office spaces and the rise of coworking environments are clear indicators of how the workforce is adapting to meet the demands of a new era, driven by the unprecedented flexibility that technology and changing work cultures provide.

As we already mentioned, these generations prioritize purpose-driven work and are more likely to seek employment with organizations that align with their personal values. They want to work for companies that make a positive impact on society and the environment. As a result, businesses will need to incorporate corporate social responsibility (CSR) and sustainability into their core strategies. Corporate social responsibility refers to the ethical framework and practices that companies adopt to ensure their operations positively impact society, the environment, and the economy. This includes initiatives like reducing carbon footprints, improving labor policies, engaging in fair trade, supporting community projects, and ensuring ethical business practices. By integrating CSR and sustainability, businesses enhance their reputations and build consumer trust and contribute to long-term economic and environmental health. This could lead to the emergence of new industries and job roles centered around social good, environmental stewardship, and ethical business practices.

Diversity and inclusion are not just buzzwords for Millennials and Gen Z; they are fundamental expectations. Research supports the positive impact of diversity and inclusion on business outcomes. A study by McKinsey & Company[9] in 2020 found that companies in the top quartile for ethnic and cultural diversity on executive teams were 36% more likely to have above-average profitability than those in the bottom quartile. Additionally, companies with more gender diversity were 25% more likely to outperform their less diverse counterparts. These findings underscore the financial benefits of fostering a diverse and inclusive workplace, beyond the moral and ethical imperatives.

Furthermore, a 2018 report by Boston Consulting Group[10] (BCG) revealed that companies with more diverse management teams have 19% higher revenues due to innovation. This correlation highlights that diversity drives innovation by introducing varied perspectives, which can lead to more creative problem-solving and better decision-making. For Millennials and Gen Z, working in an environment that values diverse voices is not just preferable but essential. These generations have grown up in a more connected and globalized world, making them more aware of and sensitive to issues of inequality and representation.

For Millennials and Gen Z, working in an environment that values diverse voices is not just preferable but essential. These generations have grown up in a more connected and globalized world, making them more aware of and sensitive to issues of inequality and representation. According to a Deloitte Millennial Survey[11] conducted in 2019, 74% of respondents believed that businesses focus too much on their own agendas and not enough on helping to improve society. Furthermore, 57% of Millennials stated that they would leave their current employer for a more inclusive one.

A survey by Glassdoor[12] in 2020 found that 76% of job seekers and employees consider a diverse workforce an important factor when evaluating companies and job offers. This sentiment is even stronger among younger workers, with 83% of Millennials prioritizing diversity when choosing employers. This underscores the importance of diversity and inclusion as critical factors in attracting and retaining talent from these generations.

As these trends continue to unfold, the future of work will be significantly shaped by the emphasis on diversity and inclusion. Companies that fail to prioritize these values may struggle to attract and retain top talent from these generations. Conversely, businesses that commit to building diverse and inclusive workplaces will not only benefit from enhanced innovation and creativity but will also be better positioned to compete in a global market.

In the future, we can expect diversity and inclusion to become even more integral to organizational strategies. Companies will invest in training programs to raise awareness and understanding of unconscious biases, develop more equitable hiring practices, and implement policies that support a diverse workforce. This shift will lead to more inclusive leadership, where decision-makers reflect the diversity of the broader workforce and society.

Additionally, the proliferation of remote work will provide opportunities to tap into a global talent pool, further enhancing diversity. By removing geographical barriers, companies can hire individuals from different cultural backgrounds, bringing in unique perspectives that can drive innovation and growth. This global approach to hiring will also help companies better understand and serve diverse markets.

Moreover, technology will play a crucial role in advancing diversity and inclusion. AI and data analytics can help identify and address biases in recruitment and promotion processes, ensuring that opportunities are distributed fairly. VR and AR can be used for immersive training programs that promote empathy and understanding among employees.

Technology will continue to be a significant driver of change, with these tech-savvy generations pushing for greater integration of digital tools in the workplace. AI, machine learning, and automation will become even more embedded in daily work routines, enhancing productivity and enabling employees to focus on more strategic and creative tasks. The ability to leverage these technologies will be crucial for businesses looking to stay competitive and innovative.

Lifelong learning will become the norm as Millennials and Gen Z place a high value on continuous development and upskilling. They will seek out employers who invest in their growth and provide opportunities for learning and career advancement. This shift will drive the evolution of educational institutions and corporate training programs, emphasizing adaptable, personalized learning experiences that cater to the needs of an ever-changing job market.

The traditional concept of career progression will also evolve. Millennials and Gen Z are less likely to follow linear career paths and more inclined to pursue diverse experiences across different fields and industries. This trend will unfold in the form of more frequent job changes, gig work, and entrepreneurial ventures. Companies will need to adapt by offering more dynamic career development opportunities and supporting employees' aspirations to explore various roles and projects within the organization.

Health and well-being will take center stage as these generations advocate for a holistic approach to work. They understand the importance of mental and physical health and will push for workplaces that prioritize employee well-being. This will lead to the adoption of wellness programs, mental health support, and work environments designed to reduce stress and promote overall health.

As these trends unfold, the future of work will be characterized by unprecedented flexibility, purpose-driven missions, and a strong emphasis on diversity and inclusion. The influence of

Millennials and Gen Z will act as a multiplier, driving businesses to innovate and adapt to meet their evolving expectations. This transformative period will create a more inclusive, dynamic, and resilient workforce, ready to tackle the challenges and opportunities of the future.

From Persons Doing a Job to Persons with Specialized Skills to Do the Job

When we consider the traditional understanding of work, it is easy to see it as a system composed of companies and individuals. Typically, companies create job postings, advertise them through various media, and hire individuals whose skills and experiences match the job requirements. This has been the norm for decades, where work is viewed as a series of static roles filled by individuals who perform predefined tasks.

However, this traditional model is rapidly evolving. In today's fast-paced and ever-changing world, the notion that work remains constant and that job roles are static is increasingly becoming obsolete. The reality is that both work and the required skills are dynamic and continuously evolving. The future of work will see a significant shift from job-oriented to task-oriented frameworks. This shift is already unfolding, driven by technological advancements and changing workforce expectations.

What we are witnessing is the rise of a new paradigm where work is defined by tasks that need to be accomplished rather than fixed job roles. This means that companies will increasingly seek out specific skills and combinations of skills to complete tasks or projects for a defined period. For instance, a tech company developing a new software product might assemble a team of specialists including software developers, UX designers, data analysts, and cybersecurity experts. Once the project is completed, these specialists may move on to other projects within the same company or take their skills to a different organization.

AI is a key driver of this transformation. AI is not only automating routine tasks but also augmenting human capabilities, enabling the workforce to focus on more complex and creative tasks. AI systems can now perform a variety of specialized tasks, providing companies with a flexible and scalable skill set that can be integrated into human teams. For example, AI algorithms can handle data analysis, customer service inquiries, and even creative tasks like content generation, thereby collaborating with human workers to achieve greater efficiency and innovation.

This shift toward a skills-based, task-oriented workforce requires a more dynamic and flexible approach to employment. Workers will need to continuously update and diversify their skill sets to stay relevant in a rapidly changing job market. This could lead to a proliferation of lifelong learning initiatives and more personalized education paths tailored to the evolving demands of the workforce.

Moreover, the rise of the gig economy exemplifies this trend. Platforms like Upwork, Malt, Shakers, Fiverr, and TaskRabbit have already revolutionized the way people work by connecting freelancers with short-term job opportunities where skills of individuals are matched with the needs of the companies and their projects. These platforms illustrate how individuals with specialized skills can collaborate on various projects, often working for multiple clients simultaneously. This model provides both workers and employers with greater flexibility and the ability to tap into a global talent pool.

One example of this new work paradigm in action is the technology sector. Tech companies often operate in a project-based environment, assembling teams with the necessary skills to tackle specific challenges. For instance, during the development of a new application, a company might require a team comprising a frontend developer, a backend developer, a UI/UX designer, and a cybersecurity expert. Once the application is launched, these team members may be reassigned to different projects that match their expertise, or they may move on to new opportunities outside the company.

In addition to the tech sector, industries such as healthcare, marketing, and finance are also adopting this task-oriented approach. In healthcare, interdisciplinary teams of doctors, nurses, technicians, and data scientists collaborate to provide comprehensive patient care and develop innovative treatments. In marketing, teams of strategists, creatives, analysts, and technologists work together on campaigns that require a diverse set of skills. The finance industry is increasingly relying on specialists in data science, cybersecurity, and financial technology to navigate the complexities of modern markets.

As we move forward, the workplace will become increasingly dynamic, characterized by fluid teams of specialists coming together to solve specific problems before dispersing to new challenges. This shift will not only enhance productivity and innovation but also provide workers with varied and enriching career experiences. Companies will need to adapt by fostering a culture of continuous learning and flexibility, ensuring they can attract and retain top talent in this new era of work.

All these changes we mention are going to drive significant and fundamental changes in how organizations are structured. Traditionally, organizations have been hierarchical, with clear chains of command and well-defined roles. Even in so-called flat organizations, there often exists a pseudo-hierarchy that dictates the flow of decision-making and authority. This traditional structure has been effective in a stable, predictable environment where job roles and responsibilities remain relatively constant over time. However, as the nature of work evolves toward a more dynamic, task-oriented model, the traditional hierarchical structure will become increasingly obsolete.

Imagine a company that no longer assigns people to specific departments or permanent job roles. Instead, employees are brought together based on their specialized skills to form temporary, project-based teams. This approach requires a radical rethinking of management and leadership. Managers and leaders will no longer oversee static teams with fixed roles. Instead, they will lead projects or programs that require a diverse set of skills to accomplish specific tasks. The composition of these teams will be fluid, with individuals joining and leaving as needed, bringing fresh perspectives and expertise to each project.

In this new model, the role of a manager or leader will shift fundamentally. Leadership will focus more on coordination, communication, and fostering collaboration among team members. Leaders will need to be adept at managing a constantly changing roster of employees, ensuring that everyone is aligned with the company's goals and strategies. They will need to create an environment where team members feel valued and motivated, even if they are only part of the team for a short period. The ability to communicate effectively, build trust, and provide clear direction will be paramount.

One example of this shift can be seen in the technology sector, particularly within agile software development teams. In agile methodologies, teams are often cross-functional and project-based, with members from various disciplines such as development, design, testing, and product management working together toward a common goal. These teams are self-organizing, meaning that leadership roles are distributed among team members based on their expertise and the needs of the project. The traditional role of a manager is replaced by roles such as a scrum master or a product owner, who facilitate the team's work and ensure alignment with broader organizational objectives.

Another example is the film industry, where the production of a movie involves assembling a temporary team of specialists, including directors, writers, actors, cinematographers, editors, and more. Each member brings their unique skills to the project, and once the movie is completed, the team disbands, and members move on to other projects. This project-based approach allows for a high degree of flexibility and creativity, as team members can be selected based on the specific requirements of each project.

In the corporate world, some companies are already experimenting with more flexible and dynamic organizational structures. For instance, companies like Haier, a Chinese multinational, have adopted a model known as "rendanheyi," which translates to "employees and customers become one." In this model, the company is broken down into small, autonomous teams called micro-enterprises, each responsible for its own profit and loss. These micro-enterprises are highly dynamic, forming and disbanding based on market needs and opportunities. Leaders within this model act as facilitators and coaches, helping teams to navigate challenges and seize opportunities.

As organizations adopt these new structures, they will also need to invest in technologies that support dynamic team formation and collaboration. Digital platforms that facilitate project management, communication, and resource allocation will be essential. Tools that leverage AI to match skills with tasks can help ensure that the right people are brought together for each project. Additionally, continuous learning platforms will enable employees to develop new skills and adapt to changing demands.

The shift toward a dynamic, skills-based workforce will also have implications for employee career paths. Traditional linear career progression will give way to more varied and experience-rich career journeys. Employees will have the opportunity to work on a wide range of projects, gaining diverse experiences and building a versatile skill set. This will both enhance their employability and contribute to their personal and professional growth.

The shift toward a dynamic, skills-based workforce will also have profound implications for Human Resources (HR) departments. As organizations move away from traditional linear career paths to more varied and experience-rich career journeys, HR will need to fundamentally rethink its approach to talent management and development.

In this new landscape, the role of HR will transform from managing predefined career paths and standardized training programs to fostering a more fluid and adaptable workforce. HR departments will focus on identifying and leveraging specialized skill sets within their talent pool, both internally and through external freelancers. This will require a shift from a job-centric model to a skills-centric one, where the emphasis is on the capabilities and expertise of individuals rather than their job titles.

With the rise of freelancing and gig assignments, HR will also need to develop new strategies for sourcing and integrating freelance talent. Traditional recruitment processes will evolve to include platforms and networks that connect businesses with freelancers who possess the specific skills needed for particular projects. This will involve building strong relationships with freelance talent pools and creating flexible engagement models that allow for seamless collaboration.

Training and development will take on a new form as well. Instead of focusing solely on in-house training programs, HR will curate and facilitate access to a wide range of learning resources and opportunities, both online and offline. This might include partnerships with educational institutions, online course providers, and professional networks that offer certifications and skill-building workshops. The goal will be to support continuous learning and adaptability, enabling workers to stay current with industry trends and technological advancements.

Performance management systems will also need to be reimagined. Traditional annual performance reviews may be replaced by more frequent and project-based feedback mechanisms. HR will implement systems that track the contributions and performance of employees and freelancers on a per-project basis, allowing for more timely and relevant assessments. This approach will help organizations recognize and reward individuals based on their skills and impact, rather than their tenure or job title.

Moreover, HR will play a crucial role in fostering a culture of collaboration and knowledge sharing. By creating platforms and spaces (both physical and virtual) where employees and freelancers can connect, share expertise, and collaborate on projects, HR will enhance innovation and productivity. This cultural shift will encourage a more dynamic and agile working environment, where diverse skill sets are valued and leveraged effectively.

Additionally, HR will need to address the challenges of managing a hybrid workforce that includes both full-time employees and freelancers. This will involve ensuring that all workers, regardless of their employment status, have access to the necessary tools, resources, and support to perform their roles effectively. HR will also need to implement policies and practices that foster inclusion and engagement among all workers, promoting a sense of belonging and alignment with the organization's goals and values.

As the nature of work continues to evolve, one of the most intriguing and revolutionary concepts to emerge is that of decentralized autonomous organizations (DAOs). DAOs represent a radical departure from traditional hierarchical business structures, leveraging blockchain technology to create decentralized networks that operate through smart contracts and collective decision-making. These organizations are not governed by a central authority but rather by the members themselves, who hold tokens that grant them voting rights and a stake in the organization's future.

The rise of DAOs can be seen as a natural progression from the current trend toward a skills-based, dynamic workforce. In a world where work is increasingly defined by tasks and projects rather than static roles, DAOs offer a structure that is inherently flexible and adaptable. They operate on the principle of decentralization, where power and decision-making are distributed among all members, ensuring a more democratic and transparent organizational model. This approach can lead to unprecedented levels of engagement and innovation, as every member has a direct say in the direction and operations of the organization.

In a skills-based approach, work is allocated based on the specific expertise required for each task or project. This naturally aligns with the DAO model, where tasks are proposed, voted on, and executed by the community. For instance, a project needing a software developer, a graphic designer, and a marketing strategist can be proposed within a DAO. Members with the relevant skills can signal their interest and be selected based on their qualifications and the community's vote. This process ensures that the best-suited individuals are chosen for each task, promoting efficiency and high-quality outcomes.

The dynamic nature of skills-based work fits seamlessly into the DAO framework, where teams are fluid, forming and dissolving as needed. This flexibility is amplified by the use of blockchain technology, which ensures that all transactions, agreements, and contributions are transparently recorded and immutable. This transparency builds trust within the organization, as every member can verify contributions and track the progress of projects in real time. The proliferation of blockchain technology thus provides the backbone for DAOs, enabling a secure and efficient system for decentralized collaboration.

Moreover, the emphasis on continuous learning and skill development in a skills-based approach is perfectly complemented by the DAO model. DAOs often incentivize members to contribute to their fullest potential, offering rewards and recognition for successful project completions. This creates an environment where individuals are motivated to continually improve their skills and take on new challenges. The community-driven nature of DAOs also fosters a culture of knowledge sharing and mutual support, further enhancing the capabilities of all members.

As the shift toward a skills-based workforce unfolds, the concept of DAOs presents an exciting frontier for how work is organized and executed. In this model, traditional job titles and hierarchies give way to a more fluid and collaborative approach, where individuals contribute their unique skills to various projects across multiple organizations. This, as a result, democratizes the workplace and maximizes the utilization of talent, as people are matched with tasks that best fit their abilities.

The adoption of DAOs could lead to a proliferation of innovative business models, where the entry barriers are lowered, and individuals can participate in multiple ventures simultaneously. This can drive unprecedented levels of entrepreneurship and creativity, as people are free to apply their skills in diverse and meaningful ways. Furthermore, the decentralized nature of DAOs can lead to more resilient and adaptive organizations, capable of thriving in an ever-changing economic landscape.

In DAOs, the traditional role of managers or leaders undergoes a profound transformation. Unlike conventional organizations where managers hold significant decision-making power and oversee hierarchical structures, DAOs operate on principles of decentralization and collective governance. This shift fundamentally changes the responsibilities and influence of those in leadership positions, emphasizing facilitation, coordination, and community engagement over top-down control.

In a DAO, leaders, often referred to as facilitators or coordinators, play a crucial role in ensuring smooth operations and effective collaboration. Their primary responsibility is to guide the organization toward its goals while maintaining the decentralized ethos. This involves coordinating efforts among members, facilitating discussions, and ensuring that proposals are effectively implemented. For example, a project facilitator in a DAO might organize and lead meetings where members discuss and vote on new initiatives, ensuring that everyone's voice is heard and considered.

Facilitators also act as mediators, resolving conflicts and ensuring that the community operates harmoniously. Since DAOs rely heavily on consensus and collaboration, facilitators need to be skilled in conflict resolution and diplomacy. They must navigate differing opinions and help the community reach agreements that align with the organization's objectives. This role is less about issuing directives and more about creating an environment where members feel valued and empowered to contribute their best work.

The role of a leader in a DAO is also deeply tied to fostering transparency and trust. Since DAOs operate on blockchain technology, all actions, votes, and transactions are recorded transparently. Leaders must ensure that these processes are clearly communicated and understood by all members. They might hold regular updates or Q&A sessions to keep everyone informed about ongoing projects, financial status, and strategic decisions. This transparency builds trust within the community, as members can see how decisions are made and how resources are allocated.

A practical example of leadership in a DAO can be seen in the decentralized finance platform, MakerDAO. In MakerDAO, there are individuals known as governance facilitators who help manage the decision-making process. These facilitators do not dictate outcomes but instead guide discussions, organize votes, and ensure that the community follows agreed-upon protocols. They play a crucial role in balancing diverse viewpoints and helping the community make informed decisions that drive the project forward.

In addition to coordination and facilitation, leaders in DAOs often take on the role of educators. They help new members onboard, explain the organization's mission and values, and provide guidance on how to participate effectively. This might involve creating educational resources, hosting webinars, or mentoring individuals. By empowering members with knowledge and skills, leaders help build a more robust and engaged community.

Another aspect of leadership in DAOs is strategic vision. While DAOs emphasize collective decision-making, having individuals who can articulate a clear vision and long-term goals is essential.

These leaders inspire and motivate the community, helping align individual contributions with the organization's broader mission. They encourage innovation and adaptability, ensuring that the DAO can navigate challenges and seize new opportunities.

The dynamic nature of DAOs means that leadership roles can be fluid and evolving. In some DAOs, leadership positions are not permanent and can rotate among members. This approach ensures that leadership is not concentrated in the hands of a few but is distributed across the community. It also allows for fresh perspectives and ideas to continuously influence the organization's direction.

In the context of a DAO, the traditional hierarchical command-and-control model of leadership is replaced by a model that emphasizes empowerment, collaboration, and community-driven governance. Leaders in DAOs must be adept at managing decentralized processes, facilitating effective communication, and fostering a culture of trust and transparency. By doing so, they help unlock the full potential of the DAO, driving innovation and ensuring that the organization remains resilient and adaptable in a rapidly changing world.

Traditional organizations, with their well-established hierarchical structures and clear chains of command, will face unprecedented challenges as the dynamics of work continue to evolve. The rise of DAOs, the shift toward a skills-based workforce, and the increasing demand for flexibility and inclusivity are compelling these organizations to rethink their management practices. As these trends unfold, traditional managers and leaders must navigate a complex landscape to remain competitive and relevant.

One of the primary challenges traditional organizations face is the rigidity of their hierarchical structures. In a world where agility and rapid response to change are crucial, the slow decision-making processes inherent in hierarchical organizations can be a significant disadvantage. The layers of approval required to implement new ideas or adapt to market shifts can stifle innovation and responsiveness. To overcome this, traditional organizations must embrace more flexible and decentralized decision-making processes. This could involve empowering teams with greater autonomy, reducing bureaucratic hurdles, and fostering a culture of trust and accountability.

The shift toward a skills-based workforce presents another challenge for traditional managers. The traditional model of hiring for specific roles and job descriptions is increasingly being replaced by a focus on assembling dynamic teams with diverse skill sets to tackle specific projects. This requires managers to think beyond fixed job roles and consider the unique contributions of each team member. To deal with this shift, managers should invest in continuous learning and development programs that enable workers to acquire new skills and adapt to changing demands. This approach not only enhances the organization's agility but also amplifies employee engagement and retention.

Moreover, the rise of DAOs and other decentralized models poses a direct challenge to the hierarchical command-and-control approach of traditional organizations. DAOs operate on principles of collective decision-making and transparency, where power is distributed among all members rather than concentrated at the top. Traditional managers may struggle to adapt to this shift, as it requires relinquishing some degree of control and embracing a more facilitative role. To overcome this challenge, managers can learn from the principles of DAOs by promoting transparency, encouraging employee participation in decision-making, and leveraging technology to enable decentralized collaboration.

Now let's shift gears and focus on the evolution of skills and the importance of adapting to the inevitable change.

As the future of work continues to evolve, we might envision a radical and provocative scenario where skills themselves become commodities, traded on a stock market-like platform. This concept, while seemingly far-fetched, aligns with the growing trend of valuing specific skill sets over traditional job roles. Imagine a world where skills are tokenized and listed on a Skills Exchange, similar to a stock market where skills act as companies. Individuals and organizations can buy and trade these tokens based on the perceived value and demand for particular competencies. This futuristic scenario envisions a platform where tokens representing various skills, such as data analysis, blockchain development, and digital marketing, are bought and sold. The value of each skill token fluctuates based on market demand, technological advancements, and emerging industry trends.

For example, consider Maria, a software developer with expertise in AI. She holds several AI skill tokens. As AI technology proliferates and becomes integral to various industries, the demand for AI expertise skyrockets. Investors recognize this trend and start buying AI skill tokens, driving up their value. Maria can choose to sell some of her tokens at their peak, making a significant profit, or hold onto them if she believes their value will continue to rise.

Conversely, imagine a sudden regulatory change or technological shift that diminishes the demand for a specific skill, such as traditional web development. Investors holding tokens for this skill might see their value plummet, leading to potential losses. This speculative market would incentivize continuous learning and adaptability, as individuals and organizations strive to stay ahead of trends and invest in skills that promise the highest returns.

The implications of a Skills Exchange are profound and multifaceted. For one, it could democratize access to education and training. As individuals see the financial potential in acquiring in-demand skills, there would be a surge in demand for educational resources and platforms offering cutting-edge training. This could lead to unprecedented investment in education technology and lifelong learning initiatives, amplifying opportunities for personal and professional growth.

Moreover, the Skills Exchange could transform talent acquisition and workforce planning for organizations. Companies could invest in skill tokens to ensure they have access to critical competencies when needed. This would lead to a more dynamic and fluid workforce, where employees are brought in based on their current skill set and the immediate needs of the organization. The traditional concept of permanent employment might give way to more project-based, flexible arrangements, where skills are deployed as needed to tackle specific challenges.

In this speculative market, skills like cybersecurity, quantum computing, or renewable energy expertise could become highly valued assets. Companies might even hedge their bets by investing in a diverse portfolio of skills, ensuring they are prepared for various future scenarios. This approach would both drive innovation and create a resilient workforce capable of adapting to rapid technological changes and market demands.

However, this provocative vision also raises several ethical and practical questions. How would skill verification be managed to prevent fraud and ensure credibility? What safeguards would be needed to protect individuals from market volatility and potential exploitation? Addressing these concerns would require robust regulatory frameworks and technological solutions, such as blockchains to ensure the Skills Exchange operates fairly and transparently.

Moreover, the psychological and societal impacts of commodifying skills must be considered. While the potential for financial gain could incentivize continuous learning, it could also create pressure and stress as individuals strive to keep up with market demands. There might be a risk of widening the gap between those who can afford to invest in their skills and those who cannot, exacerbating existing inequalities.

Envisioning the future, we can draw a parallel between the way famous European football players or NBA stars are traded based on their market value and skills, and the potential for individuals in various professions to be similarly valued and traded in a Skills Exchange. Just as the worth of athletes is determined by their performance, marketability, and the revenue they generate, future professionals could find themselves in a marketplace where their specialized skills and expertise are commodified. Imagine a software engineer with a renowned track record in AI development being listed in a Skills Exchange, where companies bid for their time and expertise. This person's market value would be influenced by the demand for AI skills, their previous project successes, and their potential to drive innovation and profitability in new ventures. Investors could buy and sell stakes in these professionals, betting on their future achievements and contributions to major projects, much like how sports franchises invest in players.

Consider the example of Lionel Messi, whose transfer to Paris Saint-Germain (PSG) in 2021 was not only a significant sports event but also a major financial transaction. Messi's market value was influenced by his extraordinary skills, his record of success at FC Barcelona, and his potential to drive ticket sales, merchandise, and brand partnerships. Similarly, LeBron James, an iconic figure in the NBA, has seen his market value soar due to his on-court performance, leadership qualities, and marketability. Teams and sponsors invest in these athletes, anticipating a return on their investment through championships, increased fan engagement, and commercial success.

Translating this concept to the broader professional world, we could see top-tier talents in technology, medicine, finance, and other fields becoming valuable assets on a Skills Exchange. For instance, a cybersecurity expert who has successfully protected major corporations from data breaches could be highly sought after. Their market value would rise with each successful project and their reputation in the industry. Companies might invest in these individuals, securing their services for critical projects, while investors buy and sell shares in their skill tokens, betting on their future successes.

This system would not only elevate the visibility and recognition of top talents but also create a dynamic and competitive market for skills. Professionals would be incentivized to continuously enhance their capabilities to maintain or increase their market value. Just as athletes train rigorously to improve their performance, individuals would invest in ongoing education and skills development to stay ahead in their respective fields.

Moreover, the commodification of skills could lead to new forms of financial innovation. Imagine skill tokens being bundled into investment portfolios, similar to how stocks or bonds are managed today. Investment funds could be created around high-demand skills in emerging technologies, healthcare innovations, or sustainable energy solutions. This would allow for diversified investment strategies, spreading risk while capitalizing on the growth potential of cutting-edge skills.

The advent of a Skills Exchange also poses interesting possibilities for career mobility and flexibility. Professionals could diversify their careers more easily, moving between projects and organizations based on market demand and personal interests. This fluidity would enable a more adaptable and resilient workforce, capable of responding to rapid technological and economic changes.

While this vision is provocative and futuristic, it underscores the potential for radical innovation in how we perceive and value skills. In the same way sports franchises and investors recognize and capitalize on the value of athletes, future markets could similarly recognize the worth of top professionals across various industries. This would not only transform career trajectories but also amplify the importance of lifelong learning and adaptability in the evolving landscape of work. As these concepts unfold, they promise to create unprecedented opportunities for individuals to monetize their expertise and for organizations to access a broader, more dynamic talent pool.

Adapting to a Changing Work Environment and Work Style

Sam glanced at his holographic wrist display, the time flickering in soft blue digits. It was nearly time for his meeting. At 53, Sam had seen the world of work transform dramatically. He had started his career in an era of full-time employment, where everyone commuted to the office and AI was a concept slowly gaining traction. He remembered those days vividly – the endless meetings, the scramble to find available rooms, the tedious task of aligning everyone's schedules, and the manual effort required to source the best talent. Those were times of inefficiency, times when Sam would often find himself bogged down by administrative tasks that sapped his energy and creativity.

Today was different. The room around him hummed with the soft whirr of AI-driven devices, each designed to assist in his work. Sam had always been a passionate advocate for AI, dreaming of a day when technology would empower him, freeing him from the mundane and allowing him to focus on what truly mattered –

innovation and leadership. That day had finally arrived. Now, AI seamlessly handled all those trivial tasks he once dreaded. Finding meeting rooms, scheduling projects, aligning calendars, and even identifying top-tier talent – all these were managed by intelligent systems that operated with unparalleled efficiency.

Sam took a deep breath, mentally preparing to dive into the complexities of his latest project. Today, he needed to gather a team that could bring his vision to life: an AI-based device and software to heal muscular issues for people with disabilities. This project was particularly close to his heart. It represented a technological breakthrough and a significant stride toward improving the quality of life for many. The task was daunting, but Sam thrived on challenges. The AI systems he had championed were now his allies, streamlining the process and allowing him to focus on strategic thinking and innovation. He thought back to his early days in the industry, working late nights at his desk, dreaming of the possibilities that technology could bring. Now, he was living that dream, leading projects that could change lives, all while supported by the very innovations he had always believed in.

Sam knew that setting up the team for this ambitious project was crucial. He needed to agree on the budget, determine the necessary skills, and define the profiles of the contributors with Alex and Hayden. Alex, a seasoned engineer, had a knack for innovative problem-solving, while Hayden, a financial expert, would ensure that the project stayed within budget and delivered maximum value. Sam's primary goal, however, was to find the best available physiotherapist to support the engineers, developers, doctors, and patients he had already contacted for his project.

The physiotherapist would play a pivotal role in bridging the gap between the medical needs of patients and the technological capabilities of their AI device. Sam had been reviewing profiles of physiotherapists who could bring invaluable expertise to the team. He needed someone who could collaborate seamlessly with all team members and ensure that their innovative device met the practical needs of its users.

Sam highlighted several promising candidates on his display, noting their impressive backgrounds in clinical settings and research. Their experience in sports therapy and rehabilitation made them strong contenders. The ideal candidate would need to integrate medical and technological insights, facilitating effective communication between the diverse specialists on the team.

To finalize these crucial decisions, Sam knew he needed to meet Alex and Hayden in person. Together, they would review the physiotherapist profiles, project plan, budget, and overall scope. These face-to-face discussions were essential to ensure everyone was aligned and ready to move forward.

As he prepared for the meeting, Sam felt a sense of determination. He was one step closer to realizing their ambitious project. Supported by AI, a dynamic team, and his relentless dedication, Sam was ready to move forward and turn their innovative vision into reality.

Sam sat in his kitchen, the morning light filtering through the windows as he enjoyed his breakfast. The aroma of freshly brewed coffee filled the air, a comforting start to what promised to be a busy day. As he sipped his coffee, he spoke out loud, addressing his home AI: "When and where best can I meet Alex and Hayden?"

Instantly, the home AI, a sleek device integrated seamlessly into his environment, sprang into action. It connected with the personalized AIs of both Alex and Hayden, scanning their schedules and current locations. Within moments, it found the optimal location and time for the three of them to meet. "Sam, you can meet Alex and Hayden in three hours at The Innovation Hub, a co-working space downtown," the AI announced. "The space has been booked, and all necessary arrangements have been made."

Sam nodded, impressed as always by the efficiency of his AI. "Perfect. Send the invites and directions."

The home AI sent out the invitations, complete with the location and best routes, directly to Alex's eyeglass AI and Hayden's handheld AI device. A confirmation pinged on Sam's own device, assuring him that everything was set for the meeting. The co-working space was equipped with all the amenities they would need, and even coffee would be served upon their arrival.

Three hours later, Sam arrived at The Innovation Hub, a modern space designed for collaboration and creativity. As he walked in, the automated system recognized him and directed him to their reserved room. Moments later, Alex and Hayden joined him, each guided by their personalized AI devices.

"Good to see you both," Sam greeted them. "Let's dive into it. We have a lot to discuss."

They settled into the comfortable meeting room, equipped with interactive displays and AI-driven project management tools. Sam started by reviewing the project plan, budget, and scope. "Our main focus today is to finalize the team setup," he began. "We need to agree on the budget, determine the necessary skills, and review the profiles of our contributors."

Alex, always the problem-solver, quickly pulled up the profiles of potential engineers and developers. "I've shortlisted some candidates who have extensive experience with AI and similar projects. They're all proficient with the latest technologies and have a track record of delivering innovative solutions."

Hayden, meticulous as ever, provided his insights on the financials. "We have enough flexibility in the budget to bring in top talent, but we need to be strategic. Every role must add significant value to the project."

Sam nodded, appreciating their thoroughness. "I've been focusing on finding the best physiotherapist available. Our company has a premium subscription to a skills marketplace, which gives us access to top talent anytime, anywhere. This person will be crucial in bridging the gap between our medical and technical teams. We need someone who can collaborate seamlessly and ensure our device meets the practical needs of its users."

He displayed several profiles on the interactive screen, highlighting candidates with impressive backgrounds in sports therapy and rehabilitation. "These physiotherapists have the experience we need. The ideal candidate will integrate medical and technological insights, facilitating effective communication between our diverse specialists."

The team reviewed each candidate, weighing their strengths and fit for the project. Finally, they agreed on a standout candidate named Sarah, whose innovative approach and extensive experience made her the perfect choice.

With the team taking shape and the project plan solidifying, Sam felt a surge of optimism. Supported by cutting-edge AI, a dynamic team, and his unwavering dedication, he was ready to move forward and turn their ambitious vision into reality. As they wrapped up the meeting, the aroma of fresh coffee lingered in the air, a reminder of the seamless blend of technology and human collaboration that defined their work.

Sarah glanced at her wrist communicator as it vibrated gently, signaling a new notification. She was a "FlexPro" — the term for the future worker, embodying the pinnacle of flexibility, AI proficiency, and specialized skills. FlexPros like Sarah navigated the professional world through skills marketplaces, where their expertise was constantly in demand for various innovative projects.

Her personal AI device, a sleek and intuitive assistant named EVE, projected the details of the new opportunity onto her augmented reality glasses. As she reviewed the information, EVE provided a smooth, automated summary. "Sarah, you've received an invitation to join a cutting-edge project spearheaded by Sam, a program manager renowned for his work in AI-driven medical devices. The project involves creating a device to heal muscular issues for people with disabilities. Your role as a physiotherapist is pivotal to bridging the gap between the engineering team and the medical needs of patients."

Sarah's eyes sparkled with excitement. The project was perfectly aligned with her values and professional goals. She had always sought to use her skills to make a meaningful impact, and this opportunity seemed tailor-made for her. Without hesitation, she instructed EVE to accept the invitation. "Confirm my participation, EVE. This is exactly the kind of project I've been waiting for."

EVE responded with a gentle chime. "Confirmation sent. The virtual meeting details have been added to your schedule. You will meet Sam, Alex, and Hayden in ten minutes. The link to the holographic meeting room has been provided, and your system is already set up for seamless integration."

Sarah took a moment to reflect on how her role as a FlexPro had transformed her career. She was no longer tied to a single employer or a specific location. Her skills were her currency, and she moved fluidly between projects that resonated with her passions and expertise. The AI-driven skills marketplace allowed her to showcase her abilities and connect with visionary leaders like Sam, who valued her contributions and offered her the chance to work on groundbreaking initiatives.

With a sense of anticipation, Sarah prepared for the meeting. She quickly changed into a professional outfit, one that made her feel confident and ready for the important discussions ahead. She then moved to her home office; a space equipped with the latest technology to facilitate her remote work.

Ten minutes later, Sarah settled into her office chair and activated her holographic interface. Within moments, she was transported into a virtual meeting room. The room was meticulously designed, with interactive displays and a serene ambiance that facilitated focus and collaboration. Sam, Alex, and Hayden appeared as lifelike holograms, their expressions and gestures rendered in remarkable detail.

"Good to see you all," Sam greeted them. "Let's dive into it. We have a lot to discuss."

Sarah nodded, feeling an immediate connection with the team despite the virtual setting.

The story above reflects many changes that work, workers, and life will face in a future powered by AI. This story illustrates the transformation of traditional work environments, the emergence of flexible and dynamic job roles, and the profound impact of advanced technologies on daily life and professional interactions

Transition from Traditional Offices to AI-Powered, Flexible Workspaces

Traditional offices were the epicenter of professional life for decades. Employees commuted daily, clocked in and out, and worked within the confines of office walls. However, the introduction of AI and digital technologies has enabled a significant departure from this model. AI-powered workspaces offer maximum flexibility, allowing employees to work from anywhere with an internet connection. Virtual offices and co-working spaces equipped with advanced technologies are becoming the norm, enabling seamless collaboration and communication irrespective of geographical boundaries.

The Rise of Virtual Meeting Spaces

Virtual meeting spaces are revolutionizing how teams interact and collaborate. Tools like holographic interfaces and AR glasses provide immersive meeting experiences, making it feel as if participants are physically present in the same room. This enhances communication and fosters a sense of community and connection among remote workers. Virtual meeting spaces reduce the need for physical travel, saving time and resources while maintaining the effectiveness of face-to-face interactions.

Impact on Productivity and Collaboration

The shift to AI-powered, flexible workspaces significantly impacts productivity and collaboration. Employees can now access real-time data, share information instantaneously, and collaborate on projects without the limitations of traditional office setups. AI-driven project management tools automate routine tasks, allowing employees to focus on more strategic and creative aspects of their work. This results in increased efficiency, faster decision-making, and a higher overall productivity rate.

Space as a Service: A New Paradigm

The concept of "Space as a Service" (SaaS) is emerging as a new paradigm in the evolution of work environments. Unlike traditional office leases, SaaS provides flexible, on-demand access to workspaces. Companies can scale their office needs up or down based on their current requirements, optimizing costs and resources. This model is particularly beneficial for startups and small businesses, offering them access to high-quality workspaces without long-term commitments. We will deep dive into this later in the book.

Co-Working Spaces: Fostering Innovation and Networking

Co-working spaces are another key element in the evolution of work environments. These spaces provide a collaborative environment where individuals from different companies and industries can work alongside each other. This setup fosters innovation, as employees are exposed to diverse ideas and perspectives. Co-working spaces also facilitate networking opportunities, allowing professionals to build valuable connections and partnerships that can drive their careers forward.

Ecological and Sustainability Benefits

The evolution of work environments also brings significant ecological benefits. With fewer employees commuting daily, there is a notable reduction in carbon emissions and traffic congestion. Remote work and virtual meetings decrease the need for physical office space, reducing the environmental footprint associated with maintaining large office buildings. Additionally, flexible workspaces often incorporate sustainable practices and energy-efficient technologies, further contributing to environmental conservation.

The Human-Centric Approach to Workspaces

As work environments evolve, there is a growing emphasis on creating spaces that cater to the well-being and productivity of employees. Ergonomic designs, access to natural light, and spaces that promote mental and physical health are becoming standard features in modern workplaces. This human-centric approach recognizes that a comfortable and inspiring work environment is crucial for employee satisfaction and performance.

The concept of human-centric workspaces is being embraced by many forward-thinking companies, emphasizing the importance of employee well-being and productivity through thoughtful design and amenities.

One notable example is the Steelcase WorkLife Center in New York. This workspace has been reimagined around the concept of human-centric design, incorporating a variety of engaging and flexible workspaces. The design includes focus rooms with different seating options, social hubs like the WorkCafe and The Front Porch, and teaming areas with visual and acoustic privacy. This environment fosters collaboration and innovation while ensuring employees feel comfortable and supported in their work.

Another example is the SAP offices in Johannesburg, which combine open-plan individual workstations with breakout areas for focus or collaboration, informal work zones, and enclosed concentration rooms. The design also includes patios, balconies, and a pond for outdoor gatherings, highlighting the importance of natural elements and outdoor spaces for employee well-being. Furniture in these offices is designed to be adaptable, with height-adjustable desks and comfortable seating options that encourage casual meetings and uninterrupted work.

These companies exemplify the shift towards creating workspaces that prioritize employee health, productivity, and satisfaction. By integrating ergonomic designs, natural light, and spaces that promote mental and physical health, they are setting a new standard for modern workplaces.

AI and Automation in Workforce Management

The integration of AI and automation into workforce management is revolutionizing how organizations operate, enhancing efficiency, and enabling more strategic decision-making. This transformative approach is reshaping traditional roles and creating new opportunities for innovation and growth.

The Role of AI in Streamlining Administrative Tasks

One of the most significant impacts of AI in workforce management is its ability to streamline administrative tasks. Traditionally, managers and HR professionals spend a considerable amount of time on routine activities such as scheduling meetings, organizing calendars, managing payroll, and handling recruitment processes. AI-driven tools automate these tasks, freeing up valuable time for managers to focus on more strategic and high-value activities.

For instance, AI-powered scheduling assistants can coordinate meeting times across different time zones, find available conference rooms, and send out automated reminders. Payroll management systems can automatically calculate wages, deduct taxes, and process payments with minimal human intervention. Recruitment platforms using AI can scan resumes, match candidates with job descriptions, and even conduct initial screening interviews, significantly reducing the time and effort required to hire new employees.

Enhancing Decision-Making Processes

AI enhances decision-making processes by providing managers with data-driven insights and predictive analytics. These tools analyze vast amounts of data from various sources, identify patterns, and generate actionable insights that help managers make informed decisions. For example, AI can predict employee turnover by analyzing engagement metrics, performance data, and external factors such as market trends. This allows managers to proactively address potential issues and implement retention strategies before problems arise.

Similarly, AI can assist in workforce planning by forecasting future staffing needs based on historical data and predictive models. This ensures that organizations have the right number of employees with the necessary skills to meet future demands, optimizing resource allocation and reducing costs.

AI-Driven Tools for Project Management and Team Formation

AI-driven project management tools are transforming how teams are formed and managed. These tools can analyze the skills and availability of employees, recommend the best team compositions for specific projects, and monitor progress in real time. For example, a project management AI can suggest team members based on their past performance, expertise, and current workload, ensuring that the most suitable individuals are assigned to each task.

Once the project is underway, AI tools can track milestones, identify bottlenecks, and provide real-time updates to managers. This allows for more agile and responsive project management, ensuring that projects are completed on time and within budget. Additionally, AI can facilitate communication and collaboration among team members, regardless of their physical location, by integrating various digital communication tools and platforms.

Case Studies of Successful AI Integration

Numerous organizations have successfully integrated AI into their workforce management processes, demonstrating the tangible benefits of this technology. For instance, several companies implemented AI-driven recruitment platforms that reduce the time to hire by 50% and increase the quality of hires by 30%. The platforms use natural language processing (NLP) to analyze job descriptions and resumes, match candidates to roles and conduct initial screening interviews.

Another example is healthcare organizations that use AI to optimize their staffing levels. By analyzing patient data, staff schedules, and historical trends, the AI system predicts patient admission rates and adjusts staffing levels accordingly. This results in a 20% reduction in labor costs and improves patient care by ensuring that the right number of staff is available at all times.

The Future of AI in Workforce Management

As AI technologies continue to evolve, their role in workforce management will likely expand. Future developments may include more sophisticated AI systems capable of understanding and interpreting complex human emotions, enhancing their ability to support employee well-being and engagement. Additionally, AI could play a greater role in fostering diversity and inclusion by eliminating biases in recruitment and performance evaluations.

FlexPro: The Future Worker

The concept of the "FlexPro" represents a significant evolution in the nature of work, characterized by unparalleled flexibility, AI proficiency, and specialized skillsets. This new paradigm is redefining traditional employment models, empowering individuals to navigate the professional world with greater autonomy and adaptability.

Defining the FlexPro Model and Its Benefits

FlexPros are professionals who operate in a highly dynamic and fluid work environment. Unlike traditional employees who are tied to a single employer and location, FlexPros work on a project-by-project basis, often across multiple organizations and industries. This model is facilitated by AI-driven platforms that match their specialized skills with the needs of various projects globally.

The benefits of the FlexPro model are manifold. For workers, it offers the flexibility to choose projects that align with their interests and professional ambitions, fostering greater job satisfaction and personal fulfillment. FlexPros can manage their work schedules, allowing them to achieve a better work-life balance. Additionally, the diverse range of projects and industries they engage with enhances their skills and broadens their professional network.

For employers, the FlexPro model provides access to a vast pool of talent with specialized skills. Organizations can quickly and efficiently assemble teams tailored to the specific needs of a project, enhancing innovation and productivity. This model also reduces the overhead costs associated with full-time employment, such as benefits and office space, making it a cost-effective solution for businesses.

The Skills Marketplace: How It Operates and the Opportunities It Presents

The skills marketplace is a central component of the FlexPro model. These AI-driven platforms function similarly to traditional job boards but are far more sophisticated. They use advanced algorithms to match workers with projects based on their skills, experience, and preferences. FlexPros create detailed profiles showcasing their abilities, past projects, and professional achievements. Employers post projects with specific requirements, and the platform matches the best candidates for the job.

The opportunities presented by the skills marketplace are extensive. Workers have access to a global job market, allowing them to find projects that match their expertise regardless of geographical boundaries. This expands their employment opportunities and exposes them to a variety of industries and cultures, enriching their professional experience.

For employers, the skills marketplace offers a streamlined and efficient way to find top talent. The AI algorithms ensure that candidates are well-suited to the project's needs, reducing the time and effort spent on recruitment. Additionally, the flexibility of hiring on a project basis allows companies to scale their workforce up or down as needed, optimizing resource allocation.

The Impact of Flexible, Project-Based Work on Career Development and Job Satisfaction

The shift to flexible, project-based work has profound implications for career development and job satisfaction. FlexPros continuously build their skills and expertise by working on diverse projects. This constant learning and adaptation keep their skills relevant and in demand, enhancing their career prospects.

Job satisfaction is significantly higher among FlexPros compared to traditional employees. The ability to choose projects that align with personal interests and career goals fosters a sense of purpose and fulfillment. FlexPros also enjoy greater autonomy in managing their work schedules, contributing to a better work-life balance and overall well-being.

Supporting FlexPros: The Role of Technology and Policy

To support FlexPros, technology plays a crucial role. AI-driven platforms provide the infrastructure for the skills marketplace, but additional tools can enhance their experience. For example, financial management apps can help FlexPros budget and plan for variable income, while professional development platforms can offer continuous learning opportunities to keep their skills sharp.

Policy frameworks also need to evolve to support the FlexPro model. Governments and organizations should consider policies that provide social safety nets for project-based workers, such as portable benefits, access to healthcare, and retirement savings plans. These measures can ensure that FlexPros enjoy the same level of security and support as traditional employees. Later in this book, we will cover some suggestions and alternatives on how governments and institutions could support FlexPros in the future.

Today's Freelancers versus the future FlexPros

FlexPros and regular freelancers represent different paradigms within the evolving future of work, reflecting distinct shifts in how work is organized, managed, and perceived. FlexPros leverage cutting-edge technologies such as AI, machine learning, and advanced analytics to enhance their productivity and deliver more sophisticated services. They often use platforms that provide AI-driven project matching, real-time feedback, and personalized skill development paths, making them more efficient and effective. FlexPros typically possess highly specialized skills tailored to emerging industries and technological advancements. They are experts in fields like data science, cybersecurity, blockchain, and advanced robotics, taking on complex projects requiring in-depth knowledge and advanced problem-solving capabilities.

In contrast, regular freelancers generally use well-established platforms like Upwork, Fiverr, and Freelancer.com to find projects. These platforms connect clients with freelancers for various services, from graphic design and content writing to web development and virtual assistance. While some freelancers have specialized skills, many offer a broader range of services that cater to a wider market, focusing on traditional sectors rather than cutting-edge technologies. Regular freelancers often work on a project-by-project basis, taking on multiple short-term assignments to make up their income, with work defined by clear, specific deliverables rather than ongoing strategic roles.

FlexPros are committed to lifelong learning and continuous professional development, frequently engaging in upskilling and reskilling initiatives to stay at the forefront of their fields. Their platforms often offer integrated learning modules and certifications to help them stay updated with the latest industry trends and technologies. Regular freelancers, however, may not always have access to such resources and may rely more on their existing skill sets. FlexPros form strategic partnerships with other professionals, businesses, and educational institutions, enabling them to take on substantial and multifaceted projects and provide comprehensive solutions. Regular freelancers generally work independently, focusing on delivering tasks assigned by clients with less structured collaboration.

FlexPros enjoy a higher degree of flexibility and autonomy in choosing projects that align with their interests and expertise. They often operate on platforms that allow them to set their terms, negotiate rates, and work across multiple projects simultaneously, giving them greater control over their careers and work-life balance. In contrast, regular freelancers face income variability and job instability due to the fluctuating nature of freelance work. They rely heavily on client reviews and ratings on platforms to secure future projects, which can be a source of uncertainty.

FlexPros tend to work on high-impact projects that drive significant business transformation and innovation, often involving consulting roles, strategic planning, and high-level problem-solving tasks. Regular freelancers balance multiple roles and responsibilities, often working across different types of projects to diversify their income streams. This can sometimes lead to challenges in managing time and maintaining consistent work quality.

To elevate from a regular freelancer to a FlexPro, one must embark on a transformative journey that involves embracing advanced technologies, specializing in high-demand skills, and committing to lifelong learning. Imagine a freelancer who begins to master emerging fields like data science, cybersecurity, AI, or advanced robotics. By doing so, they become highly sought-after experts, attracting projects that require deep, specialized knowledge. Integrating advanced technologies into their workflow, such as AI tools for project management and automation, enhances their productivity and allows them to deliver sophisticated, high-quality services.

Continuous learning is crucial in this evolution. Regularly updating skills through online courses, webinars, and industry conferences keeps the freelancer at the cutting edge of their field. This commitment to growth is complemented by building a robust professional network, forming strategic partnerships with other professionals, businesses, and educational institutions. Such connections open doors to larger, more complex projects that one might not tackle alone.

Developing a strong personal brand is also vital. By creating a compelling narrative that showcases expertise and unique value propositions, maintaining an updated portfolio, and engaging in thought leadership, the freelancer can attract higher-quality clients and opportunities. High-impact projects become the focus, driving significant business transformation and innovation, which often come with greater rewards and recognition.

Utilizing platforms that offer greater autonomy and flexibility, where project selection, rates, and terms can be controlled more precisely, further enhances this transition. Platforms that cater to high-level professionals and provide AI-driven project matching and real-time feedback help in securing the right projects that align with one's expertise.

Performance management systems that allow for project-based feedback and continuous improvement are adopted. Using analytics to track contributions and outcomes, the freelancer can continuously refine their skills and demonstrate their value to potential clients.

By weaving together these elements, the freelancer not only elevates their professional status to that of a FlexPro but also positions themselves for greater opportunities, higher earnings, and a more fulfilling career. This transformation is not just about keeping up with the present but about pioneering the future of work, where specialization, technology, and continuous learning converge to create unparalleled professional growth.

The Future of the FlexPro Model
Looking ahead, the FlexPro model is poised to become increasingly prevalent. As technology continues to advance and work becomes more globalized, the demand for flexible, specialized talent will grow. Organizations will increasingly rely on FlexPros to drive innovation and adapt to rapidly changing market conditions.

Dynamic Team Formation and Collaboration
The future of work is characterized by a shift from static job roles to dynamic, project-based teams. This transformation is driven by technological advancements, evolving business needs, and the growing importance of specialized skills. Dynamic team formation and collaboration are becoming the norm, offering numerous benefits and presenting new challenges for organizations and workers alike.

The Shift from Static Job Roles to Dynamic, Project-Based Teams
In traditional workplaces, employees are often assigned specific roles within fixed departments, working under a hierarchical structure. This model, while effective in certain contexts, can limit flexibility and innovation. In contrast, the dynamic team model emphasizes fluidity and adaptability. Teams are formed based on the specific requirements of a project, bringing together individuals with the necessary skills and expertise, regardless of their departmental affiliations or geographic locations.

This shift allows organizations to respond more swiftly to changing market conditions and emerging opportunities. For instance, when a company needs to develop a new product or service, it can quickly assemble a team of experts from different fields – such as engineering, marketing, and user experience – to work together on the project. Once the project is completed, the team disbands, and its members move on to new assignments.

Strategies for Effective Team Collaboration in a Decentralized Environment

Effective collaboration in a decentralized environment requires careful planning and the right tools. Here are some key strategies for fostering successful teamwork:

1. Clear Communication Channels: Establishing reliable communication channels is crucial for ensuring that team members can easily share information, ask questions, and provide updates. Tools like Slack, Microsoft Teams, and Zoom facilitate real-time communication and collaboration.

2. Defined Roles and Responsibilities: Even in dynamic teams, it's important to define roles and responsibilities clearly. This helps prevent confusion and ensures that each team member knows what is expected of them.

3. Regular Check-Ins and Updates: Scheduling regular meetings or check-ins helps keep everyone aligned and informed about the project's progress. These meetings can be virtual, leveraging video conferencing tools to bridge geographic distances.

4. Collaboration Platforms: Using collaboration platforms like Asana, Trello, or Jira allows team members to track tasks, deadlines, and project milestones. These tools provide a central repository for all project-related information, making it accessible to everyone involved.

5. *Fostering a Collaborative Culture:* Encouraging a culture of openness and collaboration is essential. Team members should feel comfortable sharing ideas, providing feedback, and asking for help when needed. This can be achieved through team-building activities and promoting a supportive work environment.

The Importance of Communication and Coordination Tools in Modern Work Settings

Communication and coordination tools are the backbone of dynamic team collaboration. These tools have evolved significantly, offering features that enhance productivity and streamline workflows. Here's how they contribute to modern work settings:

1. *Real-Time Collaboration:* Tools like Google Workspace and Microsoft 365 enable real-time collaboration on documents, spreadsheets, and presentations. Multiple team members can work on the same file simultaneously, making edits and comments that are instantly visible to others.

2. *Project Management:* Platforms like Asana, Trello, and Jira help teams organize and prioritize tasks. They provide a visual overview of the project's progress, allowing team members to see what needs to be done and who is responsible for each task.

3. *File Sharing and Storage:* Cloud-based storage solutions like Dropbox, Google Drive, and OneDrive make it easy to store and share files. Team members can access important documents from anywhere, ensuring that everyone has the information they need.

4. Task Automation: AI and automation tools can handle routine tasks such as scheduling meetings, sending reminders, and generating reports. This frees up team members to focus on more strategic and creative aspects of their work.

Real-World Examples of Dynamic Team Collaboration

Many organizations have successfully implemented dynamic team models, reaping the benefits of increased flexibility and innovation. For example:

1. Google: Google's project-based approach allows employees to work on multiple projects across different teams. This model encourages cross-functional collaboration and helps the company quickly adapt to new challenges and opportunities.

2. IBM: IBM uses agile methodologies to form dynamic teams for software development projects. These teams are composed of specialists from various disciplines, working together to deliver high-quality products in shorter timeframes.

3. Spotify: Spotify's squad model is another example of dynamic team formation. Squads are small, cross-functional teams responsible for specific features or services. They operate independently but align with the company's overall goals and priorities.

The Benefits of Dynamic Team Formation

The dynamic team model offers several advantages:

1. Enhanced Innovation: Bringing together individuals with diverse skills and perspectives fosters creativity and innovation. Team members can leverage their unique expertise to develop novel solutions to complex problems.

2. Greater Flexibility: Dynamic teams can be quickly assembled and disbanded based on project needs. This flexibility allows organizations to respond rapidly to changes in the market or business environment.

3. Improved Efficiency: By focusing on specific projects, dynamic teams can work more efficiently. They have clear goals and can prioritize tasks accordingly, reducing the time and resources needed to achieve results.

4. Employee Development: Working in dynamic teams provides employees with opportunities to learn new skills and gain experience in different areas. This can enhance their professional development and career prospects.

Challenges of Dynamic Team Formation

While dynamic team formation offers many benefits, it also presents challenges:

1. Coordination Complexity: Managing multiple dynamic teams can be complex. It requires robust coordination and communication mechanisms to ensure that everyone is aligned and working toward common goals.

2. Cultural Differences: In global organizations, team members may come from different cultural backgrounds. Effective collaboration requires an understanding and appreciation of these differences.

3. Resource Allocation: Ensuring that the right resources are available for each project can be challenging. Organizations need to have a clear understanding of their workforce's skills and availability.

The Future of Dynamic Teams

As technology continues to advance, the dynamic team model will become even more prevalent. AI and machine learning will play a key role in optimizing team formation, identifying the best combinations of skills and expertise for specific projects. Virtual and augmented reality technologies will further enhance collaboration, making it feel as though team members are working side-by-side, even when they are miles apart.

Leadership in the Age of AI and Flexibility

The role of leadership is undergoing a profound transformation in response to the evolving landscape of work driven by AI, automation, and the increasing demand for flexibility. Leaders today must navigate unprecedented challenges and opportunities, adapting their skills and strategies to manage dynamic, decentralized teams effectively.

Evolving Roles of Managers and Leaders in a Decentralized, AI-Driven Workforce

In a traditional workplace, managers and leaders were often defined by their ability to oversee day-to-day operations, enforce policies, and ensure that their teams met organizational goals. However, the rise of AI and the shift toward flexible, decentralized work models are redefining these roles. Leaders now must embrace new responsibilities and adapt to a rapidly changing environment.

1. Facilitators of Innovation and Collaboration: In a decentralized workforce, leaders act as facilitators rather than just supervisors. They create environments that foster innovation, encourage collaboration, and empower team members to take ownership of their work. This involves providing access to the right tools, resources, and support systems that enable employees to succeed.

2. *Adaptive and Agile:* Modern leaders must be agile, capable of responding quickly to changes and uncertainties. This includes being open to new ideas, experimenting with different approaches, and making decisions based on real-time data and insights provided by AI.

3. *Visionaries and Strategists:* Leaders in the age of AI must be visionaries, able to see the bigger picture and align their teams with long-term organizational goals. They need to develop and communicate a clear vision that inspires and motivates employees, ensuring that everyone is working toward a common purpose.

4. *Mentors and Coaches:* The role of a leader has evolved to include mentoring and coaching. Leaders must invest in the development of their team members, providing guidance, feedback, and opportunities for growth. This helps build a resilient and adaptable workforce capable of thriving in a dynamic environment.

Essential Skills for Leaders in Managing Remote and Flexible Teams

Managing remote and flexible teams requires a distinct set of skills that differ from those needed in a traditional office setting. Here are some key skills that modern leaders must cultivate:

1. *Digital Proficiency:* Leaders must be proficient in using digital tools and platforms that facilitate remote work. This includes video conferencing software, project management tools, and collaboration platforms. Understanding how to leverage these technologies effectively is crucial for maintaining productivity and communication.

2. Emotional Intelligence: EQ is essential for leaders managing remote teams. EQ involves being aware of and managing one's emotions, as well as understanding and influencing the emotions of others. Leaders with high EQ can build strong relationships, foster trust, and create a positive team culture, even in a virtual setting.

3. Effective Communication: Clear and effective communication is vital for remote teams. Leaders must be able to convey information succinctly, listen actively, and ensure that all team members are on the same page. This includes setting expectations, providing regular updates, and being accessible for questions and support.

4. Empathy and Inclusivity: Empathy is critical for understanding the diverse needs and challenges faced by team members. Leaders must create an inclusive environment where everyone feels valued and heard. This involves being attuned to different cultural backgrounds, time zones, and work-life balance needs.

5. Results-Oriented Management: In a flexible work environment, leaders should focus on outcomes rather than micromanaging processes. Setting clear goals, defining key performance indicators (KPIs), and measuring success based on results help maintain accountability and drive performance.

Case Studies of Successful Leadership Practices in Tech-Driven Environments

Several organizations have demonstrated successful leadership practices in tech-driven environments. Here are a few examples:

1. GitLab: GitLab, a fully remote company, has embraced a leadership model that prioritizes transparency and inclusivity. The company has a comprehensive remote work guide that outlines best practices for communication, collaboration, and performance management. Leaders at GitLab focus on fostering a strong company culture, maintaining open lines of communication, and providing regular feedback and recognition to employees.

2. Automattic: Automattic, the parent company of WordPress.com, operates with a distributed workforce across the globe. The company's leadership emphasizes asynchronous communication, allowing team members to work at their own pace and in their own time zones. Automattic uses tools like P2 (a WordPress theme designed for team collaboration) and Slack to facilitate communication and collaboration. Leaders at Automattic trust their employees to deliver results and provide the autonomy needed to thrive.

3. Buffer: Buffer, a social media management platform, has built a reputation for its transparent and inclusive leadership practices. The company's leaders openly share financials, salaries, and strategic decisions with the entire team. Buffer's leadership focuses on creating a supportive and empathetic work environment, encouraging continuous learning and personal development. This approach has helped Buffer maintain high levels of employee engagement and satisfaction.

4. IBM: IBM's leadership has embraced agile methodologies to manage dynamic teams effectively. The company uses AI and data analytics to inform decision-making and optimize workforce management. IBM's leaders prioritize continuous learning and encourage employees to upskill and adapt to new technologies.

This approach has enabled IBM to remain competitive and innovative in a rapidly changing tech landscape.

Building a Culture of Trust and Accountability

Trust and accountability are foundational elements of effective leadership in a decentralized, AI-driven workforce. Leaders must create an environment where team members feel trusted to do their best work and are held accountable for their performance. This involves setting clear expectations, providing regular feedback, and recognizing achievements.

The Future of Leadership

As AI and automation continue to evolve, the role of leadership will further transform. Future leaders will need to integrate advanced technologies into their strategies, leveraging AI to enhance decision-making, predict trends, and optimize team performance. They will also need to be adaptable, continuously learning, and evolving to meet the demands of an ever-changing work environment.

Skills as Currency

As the future of work continues to unfold, the concept of skills as a form of currency is becoming increasingly prominent. This idea means a shift from traditional employment models to one where individual skills are highly valued, traded, and leveraged in the marketplace. Skills become the primary means through which individuals gain employment, secure projects, and advance their careers. This transformation is enabled by technological advancements, AI-driven platforms, and the growing importance of continuous learning and upskilling.

The Concept of Skills as Currency

The notion of skills as currency revolves around the idea that specific, demonstrable abilities and expertise hold intrinsic value in the job market. Rather than focusing solely on job titles or formal education, employers and project managers prioritize the practical skills that individuals bring to the table. This shift is driven by the need for specialized knowledge in a rapidly evolving technological landscape.

In this new paradigm, skills are traded in a marketplace similar to how financial assets are exchanged. Workers can showcase their skills on platforms designed to match them with employers and projects that need their expertise. These platforms use AI to assess and verify skills, ensuring that individuals possess the capabilities they claim. The value of skills fluctuates based on market demand, much like commodities in a financial market.

Continuous Learning and Upskilling: The New Norm

In a world where skills are currency, continuous learning and upskilling become essential. The rapid pace of technological change means that skills can quickly become outdated. To remain competitive, workers must engage in lifelong learning, constantly updating and expanding their skill sets. This can be achieved through formal education, online courses, professional certifications, and hands-on experience.

Employers and platforms facilitate this by providing access to to learning resources, training programs, and development opportunities. AI-driven learning platforms can personalize educational content, tailoring it to the individual's learning style and career goals. This ensures that workers acquire the most relevant and up-to-date skills needed in the marketplace.

The Skills Marketplace: How It Operates and Its Impact

The skills marketplace is a digital platform where individuals list their skills, and employers or project managers post opportunities requiring specific abilities. These platforms use AI algorithms to match the right talent with the right projects, streamlining the hiring process and ensuring a good fit between workers and employers.

For example, a company needing a data scientist for a short-term project can post the requirements on the skills marketplace. AI algorithms analyze the profiles of registered data scientists, considering factors such as experience, specific skills, and previous project outcomes. The platform then recommends the best candidates, who can be hired quickly and efficiently.

The impact of the skills marketplace is profound. It democratizes access to job opportunities, allowing individuals from diverse backgrounds and locations to compete based on their abilities. It also enables companies to access a global talent pool, increasing the likelihood of finding the perfect match for their needs. This model promotes a more dynamic and flexible workforce, capable of adapting to changing demands and innovations.

Examples of Emerging Skills and Their Market Demand

Certain skills are becoming increasingly valuable in the skills marketplace due to technological advancements and evolving business needs. These include:

1. Data Science and Analytics: As organizations generate and rely on vast amounts of data, the demand for data scientists and analysts continues to grow. These professionals are essential for interpreting data, identifying trends, and informing strategic decisions.

2. AI and Machine Learning: AI and machine learning experts are in high demand as more industries adopt these technologies. Their skills are crucial for developing AI models, automating processes, and enhancing decision-making.

3. Cybersecurity: With the rise of cyber threats, cybersecurity professionals are vital for protecting sensitive information and maintaining trust in digital systems. Skills in threat detection, incident response, and security architecture are particularly sought after.

4. Cloud Computing: As businesses migrate to the cloud, expertise in cloud infrastructure, services, and solutions is essential. Cloud engineers and architects are needed to design, implement, and manage cloud-based systems.

5. Digital Marketing: The shift to online commerce and digital engagement has increased the demand for digital marketing skills. Professionals who can effectively use social media, SEO, content marketing, and data analytics to drive business growth are highly valued.

The Role of AI in Verifying and Valuing Skills

AI plays a crucial role in verifying and valuing skills in the marketplace. AI-driven platforms can assess an individual's skills through various means, such as analyzing work samples, conducting automated tests, and reviewing performance metrics from previous projects. This ensures that the skills listed by workers are accurate and up to date.

Moreover, AI can help value skills by analyzing market trends and demand. For instance, if there is a growing need for cybersecurity experts, the platform can adjust the value of related skills accordingly. This dynamic valuation ensures that workers are compensated fairly based on current market conditions.

Challenges and Considerations

While the concept of skills as currency offers numerous benefits, it also presents challenges. One major concern is the potential for inequality. Access to learning resources and opportunities for upskilling can vary based on socioeconomic factors. To address this, organizations and governments must invest in education and training programs that are accessible to all.

Another consideration is the potential for skills to become commoditized. This could lead to a focus on short-term project work rather than long-term career development. To mitigate this, platforms and employers should emphasize the importance of career growth and provide pathways for workers to advance and diversify their skills.

Future Predictions and Scenarios

As the concept of skills as currency continues to evolve, several future scenarios are possible. One potential development is the creation of skill-based stock markets, where individuals' skills are traded like financial assets. This could lead to new investment opportunities and financial instruments centered around human capital.

Another possibility, as we have seen in previous sections of this book, is the proliferation of decentralized autonomous organizations (DAOs) that operate entirely based on skills and contributions. In these organizations, workers are rewarded directly for their skills and outputs, bypassing traditional hierarchical structures.

To finalize this chapter, it is essential to articulate a visionary perspective on the foundational elements that will shape the workforce of the future. The landscape of employment is undergoing an unprecedented transformation, driven by the proliferation of AI and evolving gig economy dynamics. The traditional model of a fully-employed workforce, while still critical for core functions and strategic continuity, is becoming just one part of a more complex and flexible labor ecosystem.

At the apex of this new structure, we have the Full-Time Employee (FTE) workforce. These individuals represent the backbone of organizational knowledge and continuity. Their deep institutional understanding and commitment are invaluable, especially in navigating and steering long-term strategic initiatives. However, in future organizations, the number of FTEs will be minimal, focusing primarily on roles that require deep strategic insight, leadership, and essential continuity. The cost associated with maintaining this workforce demands a balanced approach, leveraging other workforce segments to optimize efficiency and flexibility.

Short-term freelancers form the first layer of this diversified approach. These professionals provide the agility to respond to immediate, short-duration needs without the long-term financial commitments associated with full-time hires. They bring specialized skills and fresh perspectives, enriching project outcomes with their diverse experiences across various industries. This segment is particularly valuable for addressing sudden spikes in workload, project-based tasks, and niche expertise requirements that are transient.

In a slightly more extended engagement model, longer-term freelancers offer a balance between the flexibility of short-term contracts and the depth of integration seen with FTEs. These professionals become quasi-integral parts of teams, providing sustained value over more extended periods while still allowing organizations to adjust to changing project scopes and business conditions without the long-term commitments of traditional employment. They contribute significantly to projects that demand continuity over months or even years, ensuring stability without the inflexibility of permanent employment.

The next evolution in workforce dynamics is driven by AI, categorized into Artificial Capable Intelligence (ACI) and Artificial Operations Intelligence (AOI). ACI refers to systems designed to perform complex, cognitive tasks that require nuanced understanding and decision-making, traditionally the domain of skilled human workers. These systems enhance productivity, ensure consistency, and operate without the limitations of human fatigue, providing a significant multiplier effect on operational capacity.

AOI, on the other hand, encompasses AI systems tailored for managing operational tasks. These systems oversee the coordination of workflows, key performance indicators (KPIs), and even aspects of hiring, ensuring that the human workforce—be it FTEs, freelancers, or AI counterparts—is optimally utilized. AOI effectively acts as a supervisory layer, harmonizing the diverse elements of the workforce to function seamlessly toward common organizational goals.

In this integrated model, AI does not merely support but orchestrates the diverse components of the workforce, enabling a highly adaptive, efficient, and responsive organizational structure. This shift toward an AI-augmented workforce is not just a technological evolution but a strategic necessity in an increasingly dynamic and competitive global market.

The future workforce will be a synergistic blend of full-time employees, varying tiers of freelance talent, and sophisticated AI systems. This model not only offers cost efficiency and operational flexibility but also fosters an environment where innovation and agility are paramount. Embracing this new paradigm will be crucial for organizations aiming to thrive in the rapidly evolving economic landscape, where the only constant is change.

These pillars form the foundation of a workforce that can swiftly adapt to market demands, leverage a broad spectrum of expertise, and integrate advanced technological capabilities to maintain a competitive edge. This holistic approach ensures that companies are not only resilient but also positioned for sustained growth and innovation in the face of continuous change.

When Companies Seek People: Transforming Job Markets

The concept of work has undergone numerous transformations over the centuries, from agrarian economies to industrial revolutions, and now, the dawn of the digital age. Each shift has brought about significant changes in how companies operate, how workers engage with their jobs, and how the overall economy functions. As we stand on the brink of another unprecedented shift, it's crucial to understand where we've come from to appreciate where we are heading.

Overview of Traditional Job Markets

Historically, the job market has been characterized by a series of well-defined steps and processes that connect employers with potential employees. This traditional model has been the cornerstone of employment for decades, if not centuries, and it is rooted in several key practices.

1. Companies Posting Job Openings: For most of the 20th century and into the early 21st century, the primary method for companies to fill positions was through job postings. These postings appeared in various forms – newspaper classifieds, company bulletin boards, job fairs, and, more recently, online job boards and corporate websites. Employers would list the qualifications, skills, and experience required for the position, along with the responsibilities and expectations tied to the role.

This system allowed companies to cast a wide net, reaching potential candidates who were actively seeking employment. However, it also relied heavily on the assumption that the best candidates would be actively looking for new opportunities at the right time, which was not always the case.

2. Candidates Submit Resumes, Go Through Interviews, and Are Hired as Full-Time Employees: The next step in the traditional job market involves candidates responding to job postings by submitting their resumes. Resumes typically detail an individual's educational background, work experience, skills, and other relevant information. This document serves as the initial filter for employers to screen potential hires.

After reviewing resumes, companies shortlist candidates who appear to meet the job requirements. These candidates are then invited for interviews, which can range from a single meeting to multiple rounds involving various stakeholders within the company. The interview process is designed to assess a candidate's fit for the role, their compatibility with the company's culture, and their ability to contribute to the organization's goals.

Successful candidates are offered positions, usually as full-time employees. This arrangement involves a set number of working hours per week, a salary, and often benefits such as health insurance, retirement plans, and paid time off. The expectation is that employees will remain with the company for an extended period, contributing to its long-term success.

While the traditional job market has served its purpose for many years, it is not without its drawbacks. One of the most significant issues is the time-consuming nature of the process. From posting a job to receiving applications, conducting interviews, and finally hiring a candidate, the entire process can take weeks or even months. This delay can be particularly problematic for companies needing to fill positions quickly to address immediate business needs.

Additionally, the traditional job market can be inefficient in matching the right candidates with the right roles. Resumes often fail to capture the full extent of a candidate's skills and potential, and interviews can be influenced by unconscious biases. As a result, employers may overlook qualified candidates or hire individuals who do not fully meet the job's requirements.

Moreover, this model often does not account for the dynamic nature of today's work environment. Job roles and required skills are evolving at a rapid pace, driven by technological advancements and changing business landscapes. The static nature of job descriptions and the rigid structure of traditional employment contracts can hinder both employees' and employers' ability to adapt to these changes.

Shift to a Skill-Based Economy

As the world of work continues to evolve, driven by technological advancements and changing societal norms, we are witnessing a fundamental shift from a job-based economy to a skill-based economy. This transition is reshaping how we think about employment, talent acquisition, and workforce development.

Introduction to the Concept of a Skill-Based Economy

A skill-based economy prioritizes the specific abilities and expertise individuals bring to the table over traditional job titles and roles. In this new paradigm, the focus shifts from hiring people to fill predefined positions to engaging individuals for their unique skills, which can be dynamically applied to various projects and tasks. This approach acknowledges that the rapidly changing technological landscape demands a more flexible and adaptive workforce, capable of learning and evolving continuously.

The skill-based economy is built on the premise that an individual's value lies in their ability to perform specific tasks effectively, regardless of their formal education or job history. This shift encourages a more granular understanding of what workers can do and how their skills can be utilized most efficiently. It also opens up opportunities for people from diverse backgrounds to contribute based on their actual competencies, rather than being filtered out by traditional hiring criteria.

Explanation of How Skills, Rather Than Jobs, Will Be the Central Focus in the Future

In the future, the concept of a "job" as a fixed set of responsibilities tied to a particular employer will become increasingly obsolete. Instead, the economy will revolve around skills and the dynamic application of those skills to various projects and initiatives. Here's how this transformation will unfold:

1. Project-Based Work Structures: Companies will move toward project-based work structures, where the primary focus is on completing specific tasks or achieving particular outcomes. Instead of hiring full-time employees for general roles, organizations will assemble teams based on the precise skills required for each project. This approach allows for greater flexibility and efficiency, as teams can be reconfigured as needed to address changing priorities and market demands.

2. *Dynamic Skill Matching:* AI-driven platforms will play a crucial role in this skill-based economy by facilitating the dynamic matching of skills to projects. These platforms will analyze both the skills needed for specific tasks and the skills available within the talent pool, ensuring that the best-suited individuals are selected for each project. This real-time matching process will enhance productivity and innovation by leveraging the right expertise at the right time.

3. *Continuous Learning and Development:* The emphasis on skills will drive a culture of continuous learning and development. Workers will be encouraged to continually update and expand their skill sets to stay relevant and competitive in the marketplace. Online courses, certifications, and practical experience will become the primary means of acquiring new skills. This shift will create a more dynamic and adaptable workforce, capable of responding to the ever-evolving demands of the digital age.

4. *Decentralized and Remote Work:* The skill-based economy will further accelerate the trend toward decentralized and remote work. With skills being the primary currency, geographical location will become less relevant. Companies will be able to tap into a global talent pool, accessing specialized skills from anywhere in the world. This will both expand opportunities for workers and enhance diversity and inclusivity in the workforce.

How AI Will Facilitate This Transformation
AI will be the driving force behind the shift to a skill-based economy. AI technologies will enable the efficient and accurate

assessment, validation, and matching of skills, making the entire process more streamlined and effective. Here's how AI will facilitate this transformation:

1. *Skill Assessment and Validation:* AI-powered platforms will evaluate individuals' skills through various methods, such as analyzing work samples, conducting automated tests, and reviewing performance data. These assessments will provide a comprehensive and objective measure of an individual's abilities, ensuring that the skills listed in their profiles are accurate and up to date.

2. *Skill Matching Algorithms:* Advanced AI algorithms will match individuals' skills to the specific needs of projects. These algorithms will consider various factors, including the complexity of the task, the required skill level, and the individual's past performance. This precise matching process will ensure that the best-suited talent is engaged for each project, maximizing efficiency and outcomes. This will result in job titles becoming completely irrelevant.

3. *Personalized Learning and Development:* AI will also support continuous learning by recommending personalized training and development opportunities. Based on an individual's current skill set and career goals, AI-driven platforms will suggest relevant courses, certifications, and experiences to help them acquire new skills and stay competitive. This targeted approach to learning will accelerate skill acquisition and career growth.

4. *Workforce Analytics:* AI will provide valuable insights into workforce trends and skill demands, helping companies make informed decisions about talent acquisition and development. By analyzing data on skill gaps, emerging technologies, and market needs, organizations can proactively address their workforce requirements and stay ahead of the competition.

Transformation from Job Markets to Skill Markets

As the future of work continues to evolve, we are witnessing a transformative shift from traditional job markets to skill markets. This change is redefining how companies seek talent and how individuals find opportunities, leading to a more dynamic, efficient, and responsive labor market.

Shift from Traditional Job Markets to Skill Markets

The traditional job market has long been characterized by a static and rigid structure where companies post job openings and individuals apply for these predefined roles. This model relies heavily on job titles, formal education, and a linear career progression. However, this approach is becoming increasingly outdated in the face of rapid technological advancements and the growing complexity of business needs.

In a skill market, the emphasis shifts from static job roles to dynamic skills. Companies no longer look to fill specific positions but rather seek out particular skills needed for various projects or tasks. This transition is driven by the recognition that skills, not job titles, are what ultimately drive productivity, innovation, and success in the modern economy.

How Companies Will Post Projects Requiring Specific Skills Rather Than Jobs

In the emerging skill market, companies will approach talent acquisition differently. Instead of posting job openings with a broad set of responsibilities and requirements, organizations will post specific projects or tasks that need to be completed. These project postings will detail the exact skills and expertise required, the scope of work, and the expected outcomes.

For example, a tech company might post a project to develop a new software application, specifying the need for skills in programming languages like Python and Java, experience with agile methodologies, and expertise in user interface design. Similarly, a healthcare organization might seek out specialists for a research project on medical AI applications, requiring skills in data analysis, machine learning, and clinical knowledge.

This approach allows companies to be more precise in their talent acquisition, ensuring they engage individuals with the exact skills needed for each project. It also opens up opportunities for workers to apply their expertise across various industries and projects, enhancing their professional development and career satisfaction.

The Role of AI in Matching Skills to Project Needs Accurately and Efficiently

AI plays a crucial role in facilitating the shift from job markets to skill markets. AI-driven platforms are designed to assess, match, and manage skills with unprecedented accuracy and efficiency, transforming how talent is sourced and utilized.

1. Skill Assessment and Verification: AI technologies can evaluate an individual's skills through multiple methods, including analyzing digital portfolios, conducting automated tests, and reviewing performance data from previous projects. These assessments provide a comprehensive and objective measure of an individual's abilities, ensuring that the skills listed in their profiles are verified and current.

2. Dynamic Skill Matching: AI algorithms can match individuals' skills with the specific requirements of projects in real time. These algorithms consider various factors, such as the complexity of the task, the required skill level, the individual's past performance, and even soft skills like teamwork and problem-solving. This dynamic matching process ensures that the best-suited talent is engaged for each project, optimizing outcomes and efficiency.

For instance, a company seeking a freelance graphic designer for a marketing campaign can use an AI platform to find candidates with proven skills in graphic design, experience in marketing projects, and a portfolio that aligns with the company's brand aesthetics. The AI system can quickly identify and recommend the best candidates, streamlining the hiring process.

3. *Personalized Recommendations:* AI also supports continuous learning and upskilling by providing personalized recommendations. Based on an individual's current skill set and career goals, AI-driven platforms suggest relevant training programs, courses, and certifications. This helps workers stay competitive and adapt to the evolving demands of the market.

4. *Workforce Analytics and Planning:* AI provides valuable insights into workforce trends and skill demands, helping companies make informed decisions about talent acquisition and development. By analyzing data on skill gaps, emerging technologies, and market needs, organizations can proactively address their workforce requirements and stay ahead of the competition.

For example, AI analytics might reveal a growing demand for cybersecurity experts in the finance industry. A company can use this information to develop training programs, partner with educational institutions, or adjust its talent acquisition strategies to ensure it has the necessary skills to meet future challenges.

5. *Enhanced Collaboration and Efficiency:* AI-driven platforms facilitate collaboration by bringing together individuals with complementary skills. For example, a project to develop a new mobile app might require developers, UX designers, and marketing experts. AI can identify the best talent for each role and ensure seamless collaboration through integrated communication and project management tools. This enhances efficiency and ensures that projects are completed on time and to the highest standards.

Challenges and Considerations

While the shift to a skill market offers numerous benefits, it also presents challenges. One major concern is ensuring fair access to opportunities. Companies and platforms must work to avoid biases in AI algorithms and ensure that all individuals, regardless of background, have equal access to projects.

Another consideration is the need for continuous learning and adaptability. Workers must be proactive in updating their skills to remain relevant in the marketplace. This requires a commitment to lifelong learning and the ability to navigate a rapidly changing work environment.

Role of AI in Evaluating and Matching Skills

The role of AI in the future of work is pivotal, especially in evaluating and matching skills. As the job market transitions to a skill-based economy, AI will be instrumental in assessing, verifying, and matching individuals' skills with the precise needs of various projects. This transformation promises to enhance efficiency, accuracy, and fairness in the labor market.

How AI Will Assess and Verify the Skill Levels of Individuals

One of the primary functions of AI in the skill-based economy is to assess and verify the skill levels of individuals. Traditional methods of skill assessment, such as resumes and interviews, are often subjective and can fail to capture the true extent of an individual's abilities. AI, on the other hand, provides a more objective and comprehensive evaluation.

1. *Multi-Modal Skill Assessment:* AI systems will use a variety of methods to assess skills, including:

> ***Digital Portfolios:*** AI can analyze digital portfolios, which include examples of past work, projects, and accomplishments. This provides a direct insight into an individual's practical experience and capabilities.

> ***Automated Testing:*** AI-driven platforms can administer tests and challenges that simulate real-world scenarios. For example, a coding platform might test a developer's proficiency in different programming languages through practical coding tasks.

> ***Performance Data:*** AI can review performance metrics from previous projects. This includes analyzing productivity, quality of work, and feedback from peers and clients to gain a holistic view of an individual's skill level.

2. *Continuous Verification:* AI ensures that skill assessments are not static but continuously updated. As individuals complete more projects and gain additional experience, AI systems automatically update their skill profiles. This dynamic assessment process ensures that the most current and relevant skills are always highlighted.

Use of Advanced Algorithms to Ensure Accurate Skill Assessments

Advanced AI algorithms are at the heart of accurate skill assessments. These algorithms analyze vast amounts of data to provide precise evaluations and recommendations.

1. *Machine Learning Models:* Machine learning models can identify patterns and correlations in data that humans might overlook. For example, these models can learn from past hiring decisions and project outcomes to predict the success of future skill matches. By continuously learning and improving, these algorithms become more accurate over time.

2. *Natural Language Processing (NLP):* NLP algorithms can analyze written content, such as project descriptions, resumes, and digital portfolios, to understand the context and relevance of specific skills. For instance, NLP can discern the difference between a developer who has basic knowledge of Python and one who is an expert, based on the depth and complexity of their projects.

3. *Predictive Analytics:* Predictive analytics use historical data to forecast future trends and needs. For example, AI can predict which skills will be in high demand based on industry trends and emerging technologies. This allows individuals to proactively upskill in areas that will enhance their future employability.

4. *Bias Mitigation:* Advanced algorithms also include mechanisms to detect and mitigate biases. By analyzing a diverse set of data points and removing biased indicators, AI ensures that skill assessments are fair and objective. This is crucial for promoting diversity and inclusion in the workplace.

Examples of AI-Driven Platforms That Could Facilitate This Process

Several AI-driven platforms are already demonstrating how AI can effectively evaluate and match skills, paving the way for a skill-based economy.

1. LinkedIn Skills Assessments: LinkedIn has introduced AI-powered skill assessments that allow users to validate their skills through standardized tests. These assessments provide a badge that appears on the user's profile, indicating proficiency in a particular skill. The AI system ensures that the tests are relevant and accurately measure the individual's abilities.

2. GitHub and GitLab: These platforms use AI to analyze developers' code repositories and contributions. By examining the quality, frequency, and complexity of code commits, AI can assess a developer's proficiency in various programming languages and frameworks. This helps recruiters find top talent based on actual performance rather than self-reported skills.

3. Coursera and Udacity: Online learning platforms like Coursera and Udacity use AI to personalize learning experiences and track progress. As learners complete courses and projects, AI algorithms evaluate their performance and suggest additional resources to further develop their skills. This continuous feedback loop helps learners stay current with the latest industry standards.

4. Upwork and Freelancer.com: Freelance marketplaces like Upwork and Freelancer.com use AI to match freelancers with projects that align with their skills. By analyzing past work, client feedback, and specific project requirements, AI ensures that the most suitable candidates are recommended. This improves the chances of successful project outcomes and client satisfaction.

5. HackerRank: HackerRank is an AI-driven platform that assesses coding skills through coding challenges and competitions. Employers can create custom tests that evaluate candidates' problem-solving abilities and technical knowledge. The AI system provides detailed analytics on performance, helping employers make informed hiring decisions.

6. HireVue: HireVue uses AI to conduct video interviews and assess candidates' responses. The platform analyzes factors such as language, tone, and facial expressions to evaluate soft skills and cultural fit. This AI-driven approach provides a more comprehensive assessment of a candidate's suitability for a role.

7. Degreed: Degreed is a learning platform that uses AI to track, measure, and validate skills gained from various sources, including formal education, online courses, and on-the-job experience. By creating a comprehensive skill profile, Degreed helps individuals showcase their capabilities and enables employers to find the right talent for specific projects.

The use of AI to conduct video interviews and assess candidates' responses is a fascinating glimpse into how technology can transform recruitment. In the future, this concept could evolve in remarkable ways, making the hiring process even more efficient, fair, and insightful. Imagine a world where AI not only evaluates language, tone, and facial expressions but also integrates biometric data and contextual information to provide a holistic view of a candidate.

In the near future, AI systems might analyze additional biometric data such as heart rate and skin conductance to assess a candidate's stress levels and emotional responses during an interview. This data, combined with advanced natural language processing and facial recognition technologies, could offer deeper insights into a candidate's personality, resilience, and cultural fit. Such comprehensive assessments could help employers identify the best candidates more accurately and reduce biases inherent in traditional interviews.

Moreover, these AI-driven assessments could be tailored to specific industries and roles. For example, in creative fields, the AI might evaluate a candidate's portfolio and creative process in realtime, providing feedback and suggesting improvements. For technical roles, it could simulate problem-solving scenarios and assess a candidate's performance under realistic conditions. This level of customization would ensure that candidates are evaluated based on the skills and attributes most relevant to their potential roles.

Additionally, the evolution of AI in recruitment could lead to more inclusive hiring practices. AI algorithms, continuously refined and audited for fairness, could mitigate unconscious biases by focusing solely on candidates' skills and potential rather than their backgrounds. This would open doors for a more diverse range of applicants, fostering a richer and more innovative workplace environment.

The integration of AI with AR and VR technologies could further revolutionize the recruitment process. Candidates might participate in immersive VR simulations that replicate the actual work environment, allowing employers to observe how they handle real-world tasks and interact with virtual colleagues. This immersive approach would provide a more accurate measure of a candidate's capabilities and compatibility with the team and organizational culture.

Looking further ahead, AI-driven recruitment platforms might evolve to offer personalized career development advice. Based on the analysis of an individual's skills, experiences, and performance in interviews, the AI could recommend specific training programs, career paths, and job opportunities tailored to their strengths and aspirations. This would empower candidates to continuously improve and align their career trajectories with their personal goals and the demands of the job market.

Future Prospects and Challenges

While AI-driven platforms are revolutionizing skill assessment and matching, there are challenges to consider. Ensuring data privacy and security is paramount, as these platforms handle sensitive personal information, and this will exponentially grow in the near future. Additionally, maintaining transparency in AI algorithms and addressing ethical concerns related to bias and fairness are critical for the widespread adoption of these technologies.

Impact on Individuals

The transformation from traditional job markets to skill-based economies is revolutionizing how companies operate as well as fundamentally changing the landscape for workers. For individuals, this shift means adapting to new ways of showcasing abilities, engaging with employers, and continuously developing their expertise. These changes bring both opportunities and challenges, paving the way for a more dynamic and responsive labor market.

Elimination of the Traditional Resume

One of the most significant impacts on individuals is the elimination of the traditional resume. For decades, resumes have been the primary tool for job seekers to present their qualifications, experience, and skills to potential employers. However, this static document is increasingly seen as inadequate in capturing the full breadth and depth of a person's capabilities in a rapidly changing job market.

In the skill-based economy, resumes are being replaced by dynamic skill profiles. These profiles provide a more comprehensive and real-time representation of an individual's skills, achievements, and experiences. Unlike traditional resumes, which are typically updated infrequently, skill profiles are continuously refreshed with new data as individuals complete projects, acquire new skills, and gain experience.

Skill profiles include various elements, such as:

1. *Digital Portfolios:* Examples of past work, projects, and accomplishments that demonstrate practical application of skills.

2. *Certifications and Badges:* Verified credentials from educational institutions, professional organizations, and online learning platforms.

3. *Performance Metrics:* Data on productivity, quality of work, and feedback from peers and clients.

4. *Endorsements and Recommendations:* Testimonials from colleagues, supervisors, and clients attesting to an individual's abilities.

Individuals Will Maintain Dynamic Skill Profiles

Maintaining a dynamic skill profile is crucial in a skill-based economy. These profiles are often housed on AI-driven platforms that continuously update and verify an individual's skills. The dynamic nature of these profiles ensures that they reflect the most current and relevant information, providing a more accurate picture of an individual's capabilities.

Dynamic skill profiles offer several advantages for individuals:

1. *Enhanced Visibility:* Skill profiles can be accessed by a wider range of potential employers and project managers, increasing visibility and opportunities.

2. *Real-Time Updates:* As individuals complete new projects or acquire additional skills, their profiles are automatically updated, ensuring they remain competitive in the job market.

3. *Data-Driven Insights:* AI-driven platforms provide insights into market demands, helping individuals identify which skills are in high demand and which areas they might need to develop further.

4. *Improved Matching:* AI algorithms use these profiles to match individuals with projects that align closely with their skills, preferences, and career goals, leading to more satisfying and productive engagements.

In the future, maintaining a dynamic skill profile will be seamlessly integrated into the professional lives of individuals through the power of personalized AI. These intelligent systems will revolutionize how skills are updated and validated, transforming the landscape of career development and job matching.

Imagine an AI that understands your career trajectory, continuously learning from your experiences and aligning your skillset with market demands. This personalized AI will be deeply connected to various training platforms, monitoring your progress and suggesting new courses that perfectly match emerging trends in your industry. As you complete these courses, your AI updates your skill profile in real-time, ensuring it always reflects your most current competencies.

Furthermore, your personalized AI will interact with employer evaluations and project updates, automatically incorporating feedback and achievements into your skill profile. For instance, after successfully completing a project, your AI will extract key performance metrics and client feedback, adding this information to your profile and highlighting your strengths. This dynamic process not only keeps your profile up to date but also enhances its accuracy, providing a true representation of your capabilities.

Blockchain technology will underpin this system, ensuring the integrity and security of your skill data. Each update to your skill profile will be verified and recorded on a blockchain, creating an immutable ledger of your professional development. This guarantees that your skills are recognized and trusted by potential employers and project managers, eliminating the need for manual verification.

The personalized AI will also offer data-driven insights into the job market, analyzing trends and predicting which skills will be in high demand. This foresight will allow you to proactively develop the necessary skills, staying ahead of the curve and maintaining your competitiveness. The AI's deep learning algorithms will continuously refine these predictions based on vast amounts of data, providing you with the most relevant and timely advice.

In this futuristic vision, the combination of personalized AI and blockchain technology creates a robust ecosystem for professional development. It empowers individuals to take control of their careers, ensuring that their skills remain relevant and valued in an ever-changing job market. This dynamic interplay between AI, training platforms, employer feedback, and secure blockchain verification heralds a new era of work, where continuous learning and adaptation are seamlessly integrated into our professional lives

As we move forward, this technology will inspire curiosity and innovation, encouraging individuals to explore new fields and continuously expand their horizons. The future of work is one where personalized AI not only keeps our skills up to date but also guides us toward new opportunities, fostering a culture of lifelong learning and growth. This transformation promises a more agile, responsive, and satisfying professional journey for everyone, aligning our personal aspirations with the evolving demands of the global economy.

Continuous Learning and Upskilling to Stay Relevant in the Skill Market

In a skill-based economy, continuous learning and upskilling are not just advantageous—they are essential. The rapid pace of technological advancement means that skills can quickly become outdated. To remain competitive and relevant, individuals must engage in lifelong learning, constantly updating and expanding their skill sets.

Several factors drive the need for continuous learning and upskilling:

1. Technological Change: New technologies and methodologies are continually emerging, requiring workers to learn and adapt to remain effective in their roles. Without personalized AIs, workers won't be able to cope with those constant changes hence personalized AI will be a must in the very near future for everyone.

2. Market Demand: The demand for specific skills can fluctuate based on industry trends, economic conditions, and technological developments. Staying attuned to these changes helps individuals remain marketable.

3. *Career Growth:* Continuous learning enables individuals to progress in their careers, take on more complex projects, and move into leadership roles.

AI-driven platforms play a pivotal role in facilitating continuous learning and upskilling. These platforms offer personalized learning paths, recommending courses, certifications, and training programs based on an individual's current skills and career goals. By providing targeted and relevant learning opportunities, AI helps individuals stay ahead of the curve and maintain their competitive edge.

Real-World Examples and Case Studies

Several platforms and initiatives illustrate how individuals can prepare for the transition to a skill-based economy:

1. *LinkedIn Learning:* LinkedIn Learning offers a vast array of courses and certifications that individuals can add to their profiles. AI-driven recommendations help users identify the most relevant courses based on their career aspirations and market trends.

2. *Coursera and edX:* These online learning platforms partner with universities and organizations to provide courses and certifications in various fields. Learners can earn verified credentials that enhance their skill profiles and improve their job prospects.

3. *Kaggle:* Kaggle, a platform for data science competitions, allows individuals to showcase their skills by participating in real-world challenges. Performance in these competitions is reflected in their profiles, providing concrete evidence of their abilities.

4. GitHub: For software developers, GitHub serves as a dynamic portfolio of coding skills. Contributions to open-source projects, repositories, and collaborative work are all visible, providing a transparent and up-to-date record of a developer's expertise.

Despite the cost associated with many learning platforms, investing in these resources is key to investing in one's future. Just as individuals dedicate time to acquiring new skills, committing financial resources to education is crucial for staying competitive in an ever-evolving job market. The unprecedented proliferation of such learning and certification platforms offers learners the opportunity to gain verified credentials from prestigious institutions, enhancing their professional profiles and job prospects.

Participation in specialized platforms like Kaggle for data science competitions or GitHub for software development showcases real-world applications of acquired skills. These platforms serve as dynamic portfolios and as evidence of one's capabilities in tackling practical challenges. The ability to demonstrate proficiency through concrete contributions and competitive performance is invaluable in a skill-based economy.

Furthermore, financial investment in education and continuous learning should be viewed as an essential component of career growth. By committing to these platforms, individuals can stay ahead of industry trends, adapt to new technologies, and ensure their skills remain relevant. This proactive approach to learning and skill development will ultimately yield significant returns in terms of career opportunities and professional advancement.

Challenges and Considerations
While the shift to a skill-based economy offers numerous benefits, it also presents challenges for individuals:

1. Access to Resources: Continuous learning and upskilling require access to educational resources, which may not be equally available to everyone. Addressing this disparity is crucial for ensuring that all individuals can participate in the skill-based economy.

On the other hand, I am optimistic as the future holds promise since the cost of computing, especially for AI, is expected to decrease significantly. This reduction in costs will be driven by advancements in technology and substantial investments in sustainable power supplies by companies worldwide.

As major corporations invest heavily in renewable energy sources and more efficient computing infrastructures, the operational costs associated with running AI will drop. This trend is already evident in initiatives by tech giants like Google and Microsoft, who are enhancing their AI capabilities and committing to using 100% renewable energy in their data centers. Such efforts promote sustainability as well as contribute to lowering the overall cost of AI computations.

With reduced AI costs, access to AI-driven training platforms will become more democratized, making these advanced educational tools available to a broader audience. This accessibility means that individuals from various socioeconomic backgrounds will have equal opportunities to engage in continuous learning and skill development. The barriers that once limited access to quality education and upskilling resources will diminish, allowing more people to participate fully in the skill-based economy.

Furthermore, the proliferation of low-cost and even free online educational platforms will be supported by these advancements. AI-powered platforms will offer personalized learning experiences at scale, adapting to the unique needs of each learner and providing real-time feedback. This personalization, combined with the decreasing costs of AI and the use of personalized AI, will ensure that individuals worldwide can afford to stay up to date with the latest skills and industry trends.

2. *Adaptability:* The need for constant learning and adaptation can be overwhelming for some individuals. Developing a growth mindset and resilience is essential for navigating these changes.

3. *Verification and Credibility:* Ensuring that skill profiles are accurate and credible is critical. AI-driven platforms must implement robust verification processes to prevent misinformation and maintain trust.

Impact on Companies

The shift to a skill-based economy has a profound impact on how companies operate, hire, and innovate. This transformation enables businesses to become more agile, cost-efficient, and innovative by leveraging a global talent pool and focusing on specific skill sets for project-based work.

Flexibility in Assembling Project Teams from a Global Talent Pool

One of the most significant advantages for companies in a skill-based economy is the unprecedented flexibility in assembling project teams from a global talent pool. Traditionally, companies were limited to hiring within their geographical location, which often restricted access to the best talent. However, the advent of AI-driven skill marketplaces has removed these geographical barriers, allowing companies to source talent from anywhere in the world.

Companies can now assemble teams based on the exact skills required for a particular project, rather than being confined to the employees available locally. This flexibility means that a tech company in Silicon Valley can hire a software developer in

Bangalore, a UX designer in Berlin, and a project manager in New York, all working together seamlessly on the same project. The ability to tap into a global talent pool ensures that companies can find the perfect match for their needs, enhancing the quality and efficiency of their projects.

Moreover, this approach allows for greater diversity in teams, bringing together individuals with different cultural backgrounds, perspectives, and problem-solving approaches. This diversity fosters innovation and creativity, as team members can draw on a wide range of experiences and insights.

Cost Efficiency by Hiring Skills for Specific Projects Rather Than Full-Time Positions

Another major impact on companies is the cost efficiency gained by hiring skills for specific projects rather than maintaining full-time positions. Traditional full-time employment involves significant overhead costs, including salaries, benefits, office space, and equipment. By contrast, a skill-based economy allows companies to engage workers on a project-by-project basis, paying only for the specific skills and time needed for each task.

This model of employment reduces long-term financial commitments and enables companies to allocate resources more effectively. For example, instead of hiring a full-time graphic designer, a company can contract a designer for a particular marketing campaign. Once the project is completed, the company can end the contract without ongoing financial obligations. This flexibility helps businesses manage their budgets more efficiently and invest in other critical areas.

Additionally, the ability to scale the workforce up or down based on project demands allows companies to remain agile and responsive to market changes. During peak periods or large projects, companies can quickly expand their teams by bringing in specialized skills. Conversely, during slower periods, they can reduce their workforce without the complexities and costs associated with layoffs.

Increased Innovation Through Diverse and Specialized Skill Sets

The shift to a skill-based economy also significantly boosts innovation within companies by enabling them to leverage diverse and specialized skill sets. When companies can select the best talent for each project, they are not limited by the skill sets of their existing employees. Instead, they can bring in experts with highly specialized knowledge and experience tailored to the specific needs of the project.

For instance, a pharmaceutical company developing a new drug can assemble a team that includes biochemists, data scientists, regulatory experts, and marketing strategists. Each team member brings a unique set of skills and expertise, contributing to a holistic approach that enhances the project's success.

The diversity of skills and perspectives also fosters a culture of innovation. When team members from different disciplines and backgrounds collaborate, they can challenge each other's assumptions, introduce novel ideas, and develop creative solutions to complex problems. This cross-pollination of ideas is a key driver of innovation and can lead to breakthroughs that would be difficult to achieve in more homogenous teams.

Furthermore, AI-driven platforms can identify emerging skills and trends, enabling companies to stay ahead of the curve. By continuously analyzing data on market demands and technological advancements, these platforms can help companies anticipate future needs and invest in the right skills at the right time. This proactive approach ensures that companies are well-positioned to innovate and compete in an ever-changing business landscape.

Real-World Examples and Case Studies

Several companies are already reaping the benefits of a skill-based economy. For example:

1. *Google's X (Moonshot Factory):* Google's X division is known for its innovative projects, including self-driving cars and Project Loon. Project Loon aimed to provide internet access to remote and underserved areas by using high-altitude balloons that create an aerial wireless network. The X division assembled specialized teams for each initiative, drawing on a global network of experts across various fields. This collaborative and dynamic approach enabled X to swiftly develop and iterate on groundbreaking technologies, pushing the boundaries of what is possible.

2. *Airbnb:* Airbnb leverages a flexible workforce model by hiring freelancers and contractors for specific projects. This strategy enables Airbnb to access top talent for areas such as software development, graphic design, and marketing without the long-term costs associated with full-time employment.

3. *IBM:* IBM uses AI-driven platforms to identify and deploy talent for specific projects. By analyzing employee skills and project requirements, IBM can quickly assemble teams with the right expertise, enhancing project outcomes and driving innovation.

Challenges and Considerations

While the shift to a skill-based economy offers numerous advantages, it also presents challenges that companies must navigate. One challenge is ensuring the seamless integration of remote and diverse teams. Effective communication and collaboration tools are essential to manage dispersed teams and maintain productivity.

Another consideration is the potential impact on company culture. With a more fluid and flexible workforce, companies need to find new ways to build a strong organizational culture and maintain employee engagement. This might involve rethinking traditional approaches to team building, performance management, and career development.

Moreover, companies must address the ethical implications of a skill-based economy. Ensuring fair compensation, providing opportunities for continuous learning, and supporting workers' well-being are critical to creating a sustainable and equitable labor market.

Future of Workplaces

Integration of AI in Managing and Optimizing Dynamic Teams

AI will play a crucial role in managing and optimizing the dynamic teams. AI-driven platforms will facilitate the seamless formation and operation of project-based teams, ensuring that the right skills are matched with the right tasks.

1. *Team Formation:* AI will analyze project requirements and individual skill profiles to identify the best candidates for each project. By considering factors such as past performance, skill levels, availability, and even personality traits, AI will assemble teams that are not only skilled but also cohesive and collaborative. This will ensure that each project will benefit from a well-rounded and effective team.

2. *Project Management:* AI will also optimize project management by providing real-time insights and predictive analytics. AI-driven tools will track project progress, identify potential bottlenecks, and suggest adjustments to keep projects on track. These tools will enhance communication and coordination among team members, regardless of their physical locations.

3. *Performance Monitoring:* AI will continuously monitor the performance of individuals and teams, providing feedback and recommendations for improvement in real time. By analyzing data on productivity, quality of work, and collaboration, AI will help teams achieve higher levels of efficiency and effectiveness.

The Disappearance of Traditional Office Spaces in Favor of More Flexible, Project-Based Work Environments

The traditional office space, characterized by fixed desks and long commutes, is becoming obsolete. In its place, we will see the rise of more flexible, project-based work environments that cater to the needs of a dynamic and distributed workforce.

1. *Remote and Hybrid Work Models:* Remote and hybrid work models will become the norm, allowing employees to work from anywhere. Companies will continue to invest in robust digital infrastructure to support secure remote work, ensuring that employees have access to the tools and resources they need to be productive. This shift will not only continue to enhance work-life balance but also reduce overhead costs associated with maintaining large office spaces.

2. *Co-Working and Collaborative Spaces:* Co-working and collaborative spaces will proliferate, offering flexible work environments that can be tailored to the needs of different projects. These spaces will provide the infrastructure for in-person collaboration when needed, without the long-term commitment of traditional office leases. They will be equipped with advanced technology, including high-speed internet, video conferencing facilities, and AI-driven project management tools, to support seamless collaboration.

3. *Virtual Workspaces:* The development of virtual and augmented reality technologies will give rise to immersive virtual workspaces. These digital environments will replicate the experience of working in a physical office, allowing team members to interact in real time, regardless of their geographical locations. Virtual workspaces will enhance collaboration, creativity, and social interaction, making remote work more engaging and effective.

The move toward more flexible and remote work environments will also have positive implications for sustainability. Reduced commuting and lower energy consumption in large office buildings will contribute to lower carbon footprints. Companies will prioritize environmentally friendly practices, furthering their commitment to sustainability.

Envisioning a Collaborative, AI-Driven Future

The vision for the future of workplaces is one where flexibility, efficiency, and innovation are amplified by the integration of AI and advanced technologies. This transformation will both change how work is performed and redefine the relationships between employers and employees, fostering a more dynamic, inclusive, and productive work environment.

The disappearance of traditional office spaces will pave the way for more adaptive and responsive work environments, where the focus is on achieving results rather than adhering to rigid structures. As these changes unfold, they will create unprecedented opportunities for individuals and organizations alike, driving economic growth and enhancing the quality of work life.

Skill Market Dynamics

As we transition into a skill-based economy, the dynamics of the labor market are set to undergo profound changes. The proliferation of skill markets, driven by AI platforms, will revolutionize how talent is sourced, assessed, and deployed as we have discussed earlier in this book. This transformation will lead to an unprecedented demand for specialized skills. The vision of a global skill market will become a reality, where talent can be accessed from any corner of the world.

Proliferation of Skill Markets with AI-Driven Platforms at Their Core

In the emerging skill-based economy, AI-driven platforms are at the heart of the transformation. These platforms are designed to facilitate the efficient and accurate matching of skills to project needs, creating dynamic marketplaces where skills, rather than jobs, are the primary currency.

1. Skill Marketplaces: Skill marketplaces are digital platforms where individuals list their skills, and employers or project managers post projects requiring specific expertise. AI algorithms analyze the skills and project requirements to ensure the best match. These platforms streamline the talent acquisition process, making it more efficient and effective.

For instance, platforms like Upwork and Freelancer.com already provide a glimpse into this future, where freelancers offer their skills for various projects. As AI capabilities advance, these platforms will become even more sophisticated, handling complex tasks like skill verification, performance tracking, and dynamic team assembly.

2. AI-Driven Skill Matching: AI algorithms play a crucial role in matching skills with project needs. These algorithms analyze vast amounts of data, including skill profiles, project descriptions, and historical performance metrics, to identify the best candidates for each project. The precision and speed of AI-driven matching far surpass traditional hiring methods, ensuring that projects are staffed with the most suitable talent.

Unprecedented Demand for Specialized Skills and How It Will Drive Continuous Learning and Adaptation

As technology evolves and industries innovate, new skills will continually emerge, driving the need for workers to engage in lifelong learning and continuous adaptation.

As companies undertake increasingly complex projects, the need for highly specialized skills will grow. Skills in areas such as AI, machine learning, data science, cybersecurity, and digital marketing will be in high demand. These specialized skills will enable companies to innovate, stay competitive, and address specific challenges effectively.

The demand for specialized skills will also extend to softer skills such as creativity, problem-solving, and EQ. These skills are crucial for collaborating effectively, leading teams, and driving organizational success in a dynamic work environment.

In the future of work, the demand for soft skills will be unprecedented. As technological advancements automate routine tasks and even complex problem-solving, the unique human qualities that cannot be replicated by machines will become increasingly valuable. Soft skills such as creativity, EQ, adaptability, and complex problem-solving will be at the forefront of this shift.

Creativity will be essential as organizations look to innovate and differentiate themselves in a crowded market. The ability to think outside the box and come up with novel solutions to problems will be a key driver of success. EQ will also play a crucial role, as the ability to understand and manage emotions will be vital for effective collaboration, leadership, and customer relations in an increasingly interconnected and remote working environment.

Adaptability will become a core competency as the pace of technological change accelerates. Workers will need to be flexible and open to continuous learning to keep up with new tools, platforms, and methodologies. This adaptability will not only apply to technical skills but also to the ability to work in diverse teams, navigate cultural differences, and respond to the ever-changing demands of the global market.

Problem-solving skills will be in high demand as businesses face complex challenges that require sophisticated solutions. The ability to analyze situations, identify issues, and develop effective strategies will be critical. These skills will be especially important in roles that involve strategic planning, project management, and innovation.

The dynamic nature of the skill market will require workers to be highly adaptable and flexible. Traditional career paths will give way to more fluid and varied career trajectories, where individuals move between projects and roles based on their skills and interests. This flexibility will empower workers to pursue diverse opportunities, gaining a broad range of experiences and continuously expanding their skill set.

Vision of a Global Skill Market Where Talent is Sourced from Around the World

The vision of a global skill market is rapidly becoming a reality, with talent sourced from around the world transcending geographical and cultural boundaries. This emerging global talent pool will drive innovation and economic growth, transforming the labor market in unprecedented ways. In this new landscape, companies can access the best talent regardless of location. This ability to tap into a global talent pool ensures that companies can find the perfect match for their needs, enhancing the quality and efficiency of their projects.

Technological advancements, particularly in AI and digital communication tools, are crucial enablers of the global skill market. AI-driven platforms facilitate the seamless matching of skills to projects, while digital communication tools enable effective collaboration across different time zones and geographical locations.

Moreover, the ability to draw from a worldwide pool of talent can accelerate project timelines and lower costs. By tapping into global expertise, companies can mobilize teams quickly and efficiently, ensuring that projects start sooner and progress faster. With team members located across different time zones, projects can essentially operate 24/7, allowing for continuous development and faster execution. This around-the-clock workflow can significantly shorten project timelines, as work can be handed off from one region to another, ensuring that progress is made even when part of the team is offline.

This access to diverse skills and knowledge can streamline processes, reduce bottlenecks, and foster innovative solutions that might not emerge in a more localized setting. Additionally, the cost advantages of hiring talent from regions with different economic conditions can lead to significant savings, making it financially viable for businesses to pursue ambitious projects.

The global skill market also holds the potential to create a more equitable labor market. By breaking down geographical barriers, it provides opportunities for individuals in underrepresented or underserved regions to participate in high-value projects and gain access to global markets. This inclusivity ensures that talent is recognized and rewarded based on skills and performance rather than location or socioeconomic background, fostering a more balanced and just economic landscape.

While the vision of a global skill market is promising, it also presents challenges that need to be addressed. Ensuring fair compensation and working conditions for remote and freelance workers is crucial for maintaining balance in the labor market. Additionally, data privacy and security must be prioritized to protect sensitive information in a globally connected environment. As these developments unfold, the global skill market will transform how we work, collaborate, and innovate, leading to unprecedented opportunities and growth.

Portable Benefits for Workers

If we look at how most companies and workers operate today, the situation is largely characterized by the traditional employment model where full-time employees receive a range of benefits from their employers. These benefits often include health insurance, retirement plans, paid leave, and various other perks designed to ensure the well-being and job satisfaction of the workforce. However, these benefits are typically contingent upon the worker's continuous employment with the company. When a worker's contract ends or if they decide to leave the company, most of these benefits cease immediately, leaving the worker in a vulnerable position. This sudden loss of support can be particularly destabilizing, as workers find themselves without the safety net they once had, scrambling to secure alternative arrangements for health care, retirement savings, and other essential needs.

For freelancers, the situation is even more precarious. Unlike full-time employees, freelancers do not receive benefits from an employer. They are responsible for managing their own health insurance, retirement savings, and other benefits, often without the advantage of group rates or employer contributions. This lack of support makes freelancers especially vulnerable, as they must navigate the complexities of securing these benefits on their own, often at a higher cost and with less stability. Freelancers are required to be their own HR department, juggling the demands of finding work, completing projects, and managing their own benefits, all without the institutional support that full-time employees receive.

In even the most advanced countries, there are limited systems in place to ensure that all workers, including freelancers and gig workers, are adequately covered. While some countries have made strides in providing universal health care or basic income support, there is still a significant gap in ensuring comprehensive and portable benefits that workers can carry with them from job to job or from project to project. This gap leaves many workers exposed to significant risks, especially in times of illness, economic downturns, or when transitioning between jobs. The current system often fails to recognize the fluid nature of modern work, where individuals might switch jobs frequently, work in multiple gigs simultaneously, or transition between freelancing and traditional employment.

The lack of portable benefits means that workers are often tied to their employers out of necessity rather than choice, reluctant to leave even toxic or unsatisfactory work environments due to the fear of losing their benefits. This system not only restricts worker mobility and freedom but also stifles innovation and entrepreneurship, as potential entrepreneurs may be deterred from starting their own ventures due to the insecurity of losing their benefits.

As the nature of work continues to evolve, driven by technological advancements and changing societal norms, the need for a new model of worker benefits becomes increasingly apparent. A system that ensures the portability of benefits would provide workers with the security and stability they need, regardless of their employment status. Such a system would recognize the diverse ways in which people work today and offer a flexible, inclusive approach to benefits that supports all workers, whether they are full-time employees, freelancers, or gig workers. This shift is not only necessary for the well-being of individual workers but also for the health and resilience of the broader economy, as it would enable a more dynamic and adaptable workforce, better equipped to navigate the challenges and opportunities of the future.

While it is obvious that the money and benefits for individual workers need to come from some source, I believe there are ways to collectively contribute to the funds necessary to ensure that workers have some level of protection as a result of their contributions to companies. This collective approach can be achieved through various innovative mechanisms that distribute the financial responsibility across multiple stakeholders, ensuring that the burden does not fall solely on individual workers or single employers.

Universal Benefits Accounts

Universal benefits accounts represent a transformative approach to worker benefits, offering a solution that is both portable and global. These accounts would be maintained independently of any single employer, ensuring that workers receive consistent contributions regardless of their employment status or location. The aim is to create a system that transcends borders, making benefits accessible and transferable wherever a worker may go, thus reflecting the increasingly global and mobile nature of the modern workforce.

To achieve this, universal benefits accounts would need to be established and managed by an independent, international entity or consortium that operates under a standardized set of regulations agreed upon by multiple countries. This entity could be a new global organization or a collaboration between existing international bodies such as the International Labor Organization (ILO), the United Nations (UN), and major financial institutions. The primary goal would be to create a framework that ensures contributions are made consistently and benefits are accessible universally, regardless of a worker's location.

Employers, irrespective of the type of employment relationship (full-time, part-time, freelance, flexpro, or gig), would be required to contribute a percentage of each worker's earnings into these accounts. This requirement would be standardized internationally, ensuring that all employers, regardless of their country of operation, adhere to the same contribution guidelines. Such a system would also address the issue of workers who frequently move between countries, ensuring that their benefits are not disrupted by international relocations.

Workers themselves could also make voluntary contributions to their universal benefits accounts. This option allows individuals to increase their benefits and create a more substantial safety net over time. Voluntary contributions would be incentivized through tax benefits or matching contributions from governments or the international managing entity. This would encourage workers to actively participate in securing their financial futures.

One of the key features of universal benefits accounts would be their portability. This means that as workers move from job to job, or even from country to country, their benefits accounts would move with them seamlessly. The global managing entity would ensure that contributions continue without interruption, regardless of changes in employment or geographic location. This portability is crucial in today's global economy, where professionals often work in multiple countries throughout their careers.

Additionally, these accounts would need to be compatible with various national regulations while maintaining a core set of standardized benefits. This could include health insurance, retirement savings, unemployment insurance, and paid leave. The international managing entity would work closely with national governments to ensure that the universal benefits accounts comply with local laws and provide the necessary coverage to workers. However, the core structure and management of the accounts would remain consistent globally, providing a unified benefits system.

To support this system, advanced digital platforms would need to be developed to manage the contributions, track benefits, and provide transparency to both workers and employers. These platforms would use blockchain technology to ensure security, transparency, and immutability of the records. Workers would have access to a user-friendly interface where they could easily view their account status, track contributions from various employers, and make voluntary contributions. Employers would also use these platforms to manage their contributions and ensure compliance with international standards.

Furthermore, the portability and global nature of these accounts would require robust international cooperation. Countries would need to agree on the core standards and regulations governing these accounts, ensuring that they are accepted and recognized across borders. This would involve negotiations and agreements to harmonize tax treatments, legal protections, and other regulatory aspects related to worker benefits.

The benefits provided through these accounts would be comprehensive, covering essential areas such as health insurance, retirement savings, unemployment insurance, and paid leave. The international managing entity would work to ensure that these benefits meet a baseline standard of quality and coverage, while also allowing for customization to accommodate local needs and preferences.

To incentivize participation, governments and the international managing entity could offer various forms of support. This could include tax incentives for both employers and workers, matching contributions to boost savings, and subsidies to ensure affordability. Such measures would encourage widespread adoption and participation, helping to build a robust and sustainable system.

Freelancer and Gig Worker Cooperatives

Freelancer and Gig worker cooperatives represent an innovative solution to the challenges faced by modern workers in securing benefits traditionally provided by employers. These cooperatives would be inclusive, catering to all types of workers—whether full-time employees, part-time workers, freelancers, or gig workers. By creating such universal cooperatives or associations, workers can collectively negotiate for better benefits and leverage their collective bargaining power to secure favorable terms for essential benefits like health insurance, retirement plans, and more.

These worker cooperatives would function as non-profit organizations dedicated to pooling resources and providing comprehensive benefits packages to their members. By coming together, workers can achieve economies of scale that individual workers could not attain on their own. This collective approach ensures that all members, regardless of their employment status, have access to affordable and high-quality benefits.

The cooperatives would negotiate group rates for various benefits, leveraging the collective bargaining power of their membership to secure lower premiums and better terms for health insurance, retirement savings plans, paid leave, and other essential benefits. This approach mirrors how traditional employers offer benefits to their employees but on a larger, more inclusive scale.

For example, a universal worker cooperative could negotiate with health insurance providers to offer comprehensive health coverage at a reduced rate, benefiting from the large pool of members. Similarly, the cooperative could arrange for retirement plans with favorable terms, allowing members to save for the future with contributions from both the cooperative and individual members.

In addition to negotiating benefits, these cooperatives would provide a range of support services to their members. This could include financial planning assistance, career development resources, and legal advice. By offering these services, the cooperatives would help members navigate the complexities of managing their benefits and career paths, ensuring they make informed decisions that enhance their financial and professional well-being.

To ensure broad participation and accessibility, membership in these cooperatives would be open to all workers, regardless of their job type or industry. Workers could join voluntarily, paying a membership fee that contributes to the cooperative's operating costs and benefit pools. Employers could also be encouraged or incentivized to contribute to these cooperatives on behalf of their employees, further enhancing the benefits offered.

The cooperatives would be governed democratically, with members having a say in how the organization is run and the types of benefits offered. This democratic governance structure ensures that the cooperatives remain responsive to the needs and priorities of their members, adapting to changing circumstances and evolving demands.

To support the establishment and growth of these cooperatives, governments, and other institutions could provide initial funding, tax incentives, and regulatory support. This would help the cooperatives build a strong foundation and attract a broad membership base. Over time, as the cooperatives grow and stabilize, they would become self-sustaining through membership fees and negotiated benefits.

Furthermore, these cooperatives would operate on advanced digital platforms to manage member benefits, contributions, and communications efficiently. These platforms would offer user-friendly interfaces where members can easily access their benefit information, make contributions, and receive updates from the cooperative. By leveraging technology, the cooperatives can ensure transparency, accountability, and seamless service delivery.

Global Framework for Portable Benefits

Government-sponsored portable benefits programs represent a visionary approach to ensuring that all workers, regardless of employment status, have access to essential benefits. These programs would be designed to provide a baseline of benefits universally, reducing dependency on individual employers and addressing the vulnerabilities faced by freelancers, gig workers, part-time employees, and traditional full-time workers alike. The key to this approach is international cooperation and a global framework that ensures the portability and universality of these benefits.

A truly effective government-sponsored portable benefits program would require a global framework, supported by an international agreement on funding and implementation. This framework would be established through cooperation among governments, international organizations, and relevant stakeholders. The aim would be to create a system where benefits are consistent and portable across borders, ensuring that workers' rights and protections are upheld no matter where they work or live.

Components of the Program

1. Universal Healthcare: Universal healthcare would form the cornerstone of the portable benefits program. Every worker, regardless of employment status or location, would have access to comprehensive healthcare services. This would include preventive care, emergency services, hospital care, prescription of medications, mental health services, and long-term care.

The funding for universal healthcare would come from a combination of international taxation agreements and contributions from national governments. The global framework would ensure that healthcare standards are consistent, providing equitable access to high-quality medical care worldwide.

2. Basic Retirement Plan: A basic retirement plan would ensure that all workers can save for their future, providing financial security in retirement. Contributions to the retirement plan would be mandatory, with a percentage of income allocated to individual retirement accounts. These accounts would be managed by an international body to ensure portability and consistency across different countries.

The retirement plan would include mechanisms for both employer and employee contributions, supplemented by government subsidies to ensure that even low-income workers can build a sufficient retirement fund. This approach would help reduce poverty among the elderly and provide a stable financial foundation for all retirees.

3. Paid Family Leave: Paid family leave is essential for supporting workers during critical life events, such as the birth or adoption of a child, serious illness, or caregiving responsibilities. The portable benefits program would guarantee a certain amount of paid leave for all workers, regardless of their employment status or location.

Funding for paid family leave would come from a global pool, supported by international taxation and contributions from participating countries. This ensures that workers can take the necessary leave without financial hardship, promoting better work-life balance and overall well-being.

Global Agreement on Funding

To support these programs, a global agreement on taxation and funding would be essential. This agreement would involve:

1. *International Taxation:* A standardized international tax system would be established to fund the portable benefits program. This could include a global tax on corporate profits, financial transactions, and other sources of revenue. The tax would be designed to ensure fair contributions from all countries and multinational corporations, reflecting their role in the global economy.

2. *Equitable Distribution of Funds:* The funds collected through international taxation would be managed by a global body, such as an expanded and restructured International Labour Organization (ILO) or a new entity specifically created for this purpose. This body would oversee the equitable distribution of funds to ensure that all participating countries receive the necessary resources to implement and maintain the benefits programs.

3. *Transparency and Accountability:* To ensure that the funds are used effectively and ethically, the global managing body would operate with full transparency and accountability. Regular audits, public reporting, and stakeholder involvement would be key components of the governance structure. This would build trust

and ensure that the programs meet their objectives without financial mismanagement or corruption.

Implementation and Administration

The implementation of government-sponsored portable benefits programs would involve several key steps:

1. *Policy Development:* Governments, international organizations, and stakeholders would collaborate to develop comprehensive policies outlining the scope, funding, and administration of the benefits programs. These policies would establish the legal and regulatory framework necessary for effective implementation.

2. *Global Infrastructure:* An international infrastructure would be created to manage the programs, including data systems to track contributions, benefits, and eligibility. This infrastructure would leverage advanced technology, such as blockchain, to ensure security, transparency, and efficiency.

3. *Public Awareness and Education:* To ensure widespread understanding and participation, extensive public awareness campaigns and educational programs would be conducted. Workers, employers, and the general public would be informed about their rights, responsibilities, and the benefits available to them.

4. *Continuous Evaluation and Improvement:* The programs would be subject to ongoing evaluation and improvement to ensure they remain effective and responsive to changing needs. Feedback mechanisms, regular reviews, and adaptation to emerging challenges would be integral to the program's success.

Visionary Legislative Framework for Benefit Portability

In the future, envision a world where the legislative framework for benefit portability ensures that every worker, regardless of their employment status, enjoys robust and consistent benefits. This forward-thinking approach involves enacting comprehensive laws that mandate employers to contribute to a portable benefits system. This transformative framework would fundamentally redefine the employer-employee relationship, making benefits a universal right rather than a conditional perk tied to a specific job or company.

Imagine a global legislative landscape where every employer, from multinational corporations to small local businesses, is required to contribute a percentage of each worker's salary into a universally accessible benefits fund. This system would encompass full-time employees, part-time workers, freelancers, and gig workers, ensuring that all individuals receive equitable contributions toward their benefits. The legislation would be designed to reflect the realities of the modern workforce, where people frequently move between jobs, roles, and even industries, demanding a flexible and portable benefits system.

The contributions from employers would flow into a centralized benefits fund managed by an international entity. This entity would operate under a unified set of global standards, ensuring that contributions are fairly assessed and distributed. The system would leverage advanced AI and blockchain technologies to track contributions in real time, maintain secure records, and provide transparent reporting to both employers and workers. This would ensure that every dollar contributed is accounted for and directed toward enhancing workers' benefits.

In this futuristic vision, the laws would mandate not only the financial contributions but also the seamless integration of benefits across different countries and industries. Workers could move from one job to another, or even relocate internationally, without worrying about losing their benefits. The portability of these benefits would be guaranteed by the global legislative framework, providing a safety net that follows the workers wherever they go. This system would eliminate the current disparities between traditional employees and freelancers, offering a level playing field where everyone has access to healthcare, retirement savings, paid leave, and other essential benefits.

The legislative framework would also include provisions for periodic adjustments based on economic conditions, ensuring that the contributions remain fair and sustainable. For example, during times of economic prosperity, the contribution rates might be increased to build a stronger benefits reserve. Conversely, during economic downturns, the rates might be adjusted to alleviate financial pressure on businesses while still maintaining the core benefits for workers. This dynamic approach would ensure the long-term viability of the system, adapting to changing economic landscapes.

To foster compliance and accountability, the framework would include stringent penalties for non-compliance, along with incentives for companies that exceed the minimum contribution requirements. Employers who consistently contribute beyond the mandated percentage or offer additional benefits could receive tax breaks or other financial incentives. Conversely, companies that fail to comply with the legislation would face fines and sanctions, ensuring that all businesses uphold their responsibilities toward their workers.

This visionary legislative framework would also encourage innovation and customization within the benefits system. Employers and benefits providers could develop tailored benefits packages that cater to the diverse needs of the workforce. For instance, workers in tech industries might receive enhanced benefits related to professional development and mental health, while those in manual labor sectors might receive additional health and safety coverage. The flexibility of the system would allow for these customizations, ensuring that benefits are relevant and valuable to each worker.

Moreover, the integration of AI-driven platforms would provide personalized recommendations to workers, helping them make informed decisions about their benefits. Workers could access real-time insights into their benefits status, projected retirement savings, healthcare options, and more. These platforms would also facilitate the easy transfer and management of benefits as workers transition between jobs, further enhancing the portability and accessibility of the system.

The impact of this legislative framework would be profound, leading to a more equitable and resilient workforce. Workers would no longer be tethered to a specific job or employer out of fear of losing their benefits. This freedom would encourage greater mobility, innovation, and entrepreneurial activity, as individuals feel empowered to pursue new opportunities without sacrificing their financial security. The overall quality of life for workers would improve, with enhanced access to healthcare, retirement savings, and other critical benefits.

Redefining Education for Tomorrow's Job Market

In the future I envision, learning will undergo a radical transformation driven by technological advancements, evolving societal needs, and the demand for more flexible, personalized, and engaging educational experiences. Future learning environments will be highly immersive and interactive, leveraging VR and AR to create engaging educational experiences. Students will be able to explore historical events, scientific phenomena, and complex concepts in a 3D interactive space. For instance, a history class could involve a VR tour of ancient Rome, while a biology lesson might allow students to virtually dissect a frog or explore the human body at a cellular level. These technologies will make learning more engaging and effective by allowing students to experience and interact with the material in ways that were previously unimaginable.

AI will play a crucial role in personalizing education. AI-driven tutors will assess each student's strengths, weaknesses, learning styles, and interests to create customized learning paths. These AI tutors will provide real-time feedback, suggest additional resources, and adjust the pace and difficulty of lessons to ensure optimal learning. Students will no longer be bound by the one-size-fits-all approach; instead, they will have tailored educational experiences that cater to their unique needs and goals.

The concept of education will extend beyond the traditional school years, evolving into a lifelong pursuit of knowledge and skill development. Continuous learning will be the norm, with individuals regularly updating their skills to keep pace with technological advancements and market demands. Micro-credentials and digital badges will become increasingly popular, allowing learners to quickly acquire and showcase new skills. Online platforms will offer a vast array of courses, from technical skills to soft skills, enabling individuals to learn at their own pace and convenience.

Geographical boundaries will become irrelevant as learning goes global. Students from different parts of the world will collaborate on projects, participate in discussions, and share diverse perspectives, fostering a truly global learning community. Language barriers will be minimized through real-time translation tools, allowing seamless communication and collaboration. These global classrooms will prepare students for a connected world, enhancing their cultural awareness and global competencies.

Gamification and edutainment will be integral to future learning, making education more fun and engaging. Learning platforms will incorporate game mechanics, such as points, badges, leaderboards, and challenges, to motivate students and enhance their engagement. Educational content will be delivered through interactive games, simulations, and storytelling, blurring the lines between learning and entertainment. This approach will make complex subjects more accessible and enjoyable, increasing retention and understanding.

The future will see a seamless integration of learning and work, with education becoming more practical and directly aligned with career development. Companies will partner with educational institutions to offer work-integrated learning experiences, such as internships, co-op programs, and apprenticeships. These experiences will allow students to apply their knowledge in real-world settings, gain valuable industry experience, and build professional networks. Continuous professional development will be supported by on-the-job training programs, online courses, and industry certifications.

Educational institutions will transform into smart campuses, leveraging the IoT and big data to enhance the learning experience. Sensors and connected devices will monitor various aspects of the learning environment, from classroom occupancy to student engagement levels. Learning analytics will provide insights into student performance, helping educators identify areas where students are struggling and tailor their teaching strategies accordingly. This data-driven approach will improve educational outcomes and ensure that no student is left behind.

Future education will prioritize ethics and inclusivity, ensuring that all students have equal access to high-quality learning opportunities. Efforts will be made to bridge the digital divide, providing necessary technology and internet access to underserved communities. Ethical considerations will guide the development and implementation of educational technologies, ensuring that AI algorithms are fair and unbiased. Education will also focus on teaching ethical reasoning and social responsibility, preparing students to navigate the complexities of the modern world with integrity and empathy.

Evolution of Educational Models: From Traditional to Future-Focused

Education has always been a cornerstone of societal development, shaping the minds and futures of generations. Historically, traditional educational systems were designed during the Industrial Revolution to meet the needs of a growing industrial economy. These systems were structured, uniform, and hierarchical, focusing on rote memorization, standardized testing, and a one-size-fits-all curriculum. Schools operated within rigid timetables, with students progressing through a series of grade levels based on age rather than ability. The primary goal was to produce a workforce with basic literacy, numeracy, and compliance, ready to enter factories and offices where repetitive tasks and strict hierarchies were the norm.

However, these traditional educational systems had significant limitations. They often stifled creativity and critical thinking, as the emphasis was on absorbing information rather than understanding and applying knowledge. Individual learning styles and interests were largely ignored, leading to disengagement and underachievement among many students. Furthermore, the static nature of the curriculum failed to keep pace with the rapidly changing technological and economic landscape, leaving students ill-prepared for the demands of the modern workforce.

As the 21st century unfolded, it became increasingly clear that traditional education models were inadequate for preparing students for the complexities of contemporary life and work. This realization prompted a shift toward more modern educational models that emphasize lifelong learning and adaptability. These new models recognize that education should not end with formal schooling but continue throughout an individual's life. Lifelong learning encourages continuous skill development, critical thinking, and adaptability, essential traits in a world where technological advancements and economic shifts are constant.

One of the most significant developments in modern education has been the rise of online learning platforms. These platforms, such as Coursera, edX, and Khan Academy, offer a vast array of courses that learners can access from anywhere in the world. They provide flexibility in terms of time and pace, allowing individuals to learn at their convenience. This accessibility has democratized education, breaking down barriers related to geography, cost, and social background. Online learning platforms also support the concept of micro-credentials, which are smaller, focused certifications that validate specific skills or knowledge areas. Unlike traditional degrees, micro-credentials are more adaptable to the changing job market, enabling learners to quickly acquire and demonstrate new competencies.

Flexible learning pathways have also emerged as a vital component of future-focused education. These pathways allow students to customize their educational journeys based on their interests, strengths, and career goals. Instead of following a predetermined curriculum, learners can choose from a variety of subjects and modes of learning, including project-based learning, internships, and real-world problem-solving. This approach fosters a more engaged and motivated student body, as individuals can pursue their passions and see the direct relevance of their studies to their future careers.

Innovative educational institutions and programs are at the forefront of this transition from traditional to future-focused education. For example, the Minerva University offers a radically different undergraduate experience, with a curriculum designed around active learning and global immersion. Students live and study in different cities around the world, engaging with diverse cultures and perspectives while tackling real-world challenges. Similarly, Finland's education system has garnered international acclaim for its emphasis on creativity, collaboration, and student well-being. Finnish schools prioritize experiential learning, critical thinking, and the development of social and emotional skills, creating a holistic educational environment that prepares students for the complexities of modern life.

Another example is the Olin College of Engineering in the United States, which integrates engineering education with entrepreneurship, design thinking, and the liberal arts. Olin's project-based curriculum encourages students to work on real-world problems in interdisciplinary teams, fostering a culture of innovation and collaboration. The school's emphasis on hands-on learning and industry partnerships ensures that graduates are not only technically proficient but also equipped with the critical thinking and problem-solving skills needed to thrive in a rapidly evolving job market.

As we continue to redefine education for the future, it is clear that the focus must be on flexibility, personalization, and lifelong learning. By embracing these principles, we can create educational systems that not only prepare individuals for the jobs of tomorrow but also empower them to lead fulfilling, adaptive, and innovative lives. The evolution from traditional to future-focused education is not just a response to changing economic demands but a recognition of the diverse ways in which people learn and grow. It is an ongoing journey toward creating a more inclusive, dynamic, and resilient society.

Skills for the Future: Beyond Technical Knowledge

As we look toward the future, it is evident that the skills needed for tomorrow's job market extend far beyond technical knowledge. While proficiency in areas like coding, data analysis, and engineering remains crucial, there is an increasing emphasis on a broader set of competencies that prepare individuals to navigate a complex, interconnected, and rapidly evolving world.

Identifying these key skills and understanding their importance is essential for designing educational programs that can equip learners with the tools they need to succeed.

Digital literacy stands at the forefront of future skills. As technology becomes an integral part of nearly every industry, the ability to understand and leverage digital tools is paramount. This includes not just basic computer skills, but also the ability to work with advanced software, understand data analytics, and navigate the digital landscape with confidence and security. Digital literacy enables individuals to adapt to new technologies, stay competitive in the job market, and innovate within their fields.

However, technical skills alone are not sufficient. Critical thinking and creativity are increasingly recognized as vital for problem-solving and innovation. Critical thinking involves the ability to analyze information objectively, make reasoned judgments, and approach problems from multiple angles. Creativity, on the other hand, is the ability to think outside the box, generate novel ideas, and apply them in practical ways. Together, these skills enable individuals to tackle complex challenges, drive innovation, and contribute to the growth of their organizations and industries.

EQ is another critical skill for the future. EQ encompasses the ability to understand and manage one's own emotions, as well as empathize with and navigate the emotions of others. High EQ is linked to better teamwork, leadership, and interpersonal relationships, making it indispensable in a collaborative work environment. As automation and AI take over more routine tasks, the uniquely human ability to connect, motivate, and lead will become even more valuable.

Interdisciplinary skills are also becoming increasingly important. The ability to integrate knowledge from different fields and apply it in various contexts is essential in a world where problems are rarely confined to a single discipline. For instance, solving environmental issues requires knowledge of science, technology, policy, and social behavior. By fostering interdisciplinary skills, educational programs can prepare students to approach problems holistically, draw on diverse perspectives, and innovate at the intersections of different fields.

Soft skills such as communication, collaboration, and leadership are growing in significance as well. Effective communication is crucial for conveying ideas, building relationships, and facilitating teamwork. Collaboration skills enable individuals to work effectively in teams, leveraging diverse skills and perspectives to achieve common goals. Leadership involves not only guiding and inspiring others but also fostering an inclusive and supportive work environment. These skills are essential for creating productive, harmonious, and innovative workplaces.

Educational programs must adapt to integrate these key skills into their curricula. Project-based learning is one effective approach. By working on real-world projects, students can apply their knowledge, develop problem-solving skills, and experience the complexities of collaborative work. This hands-on approach encourages active learning, critical thinking, and creativity, allowing students to see the tangible impact of their efforts.

Internships and co-op programs provide another valuable opportunity for skill development. By working in real-world settings, students gain practical experience, build professional networks, and develop a deeper understanding of their fields. These experiences help bridge the gap between theoretical knowledge and practical application, preparing students for the demands of the job market.

Real-world problem-solving can also be integrated into educational programs through partnerships with industry and community organizations. By collaborating on projects that address real societal challenges, students can develop interdisciplinary skills, apply their learning in meaningful ways, and make a positive impact. Such partnerships also provide valuable insights into industry needs, ensuring that educational programs remain relevant and aligned with the evolving job market.

Incorporating these skills into educational curricula requires a shift from traditional teaching methods to more dynamic, interactive, and student-centered approaches. Educators must be trained to foster these skills, using techniques that encourage active learning, critical thinking, and collaboration. Schools and universities need to create environments that support innovation, risk-taking, and the free exchange of ideas.

Preparing for tomorrow's job market requires a holistic approach to education that goes beyond technical knowledge. By emphasizing digital literacy, critical thinking, creativity, EQ, interdisciplinary skills, and soft skills, educational programs can equip learners with the competencies they need to thrive in a rapidly changing world. Through project-based learning, internships, and real-world problem-solving, students can develop these skills in practical, meaningful ways, ensuring they are ready to meet the challenges and seize the opportunities of the future.

Networking and Personal Branding: Building a Professional Presence

In the increasingly globalized and interconnected job market, networking and personal branding have become critical components of career development. The ability to build and maintain a robust professional network can open doors to opportunities that might otherwise remain inaccessible. Networking goes beyond merely meeting people; it involves cultivating meaningful relationships that can provide support, guidance, and collaboration throughout one's career. As the nature of work continues to evolve, the significance of a well-crafted professional presence cannot be overstated.

Networking in today's job market is essential for several reasons. It enables individuals to stay informed about industry trends, job openings, and emerging opportunities. A strong network can provide valuable insights and advice, helping individuals navigate their career paths more effectively. Furthermore, networking fosters a sense of community and belonging, which can be particularly important in a world where remote work and digital interactions are becoming the norm. The ability to connect with professionals across the globe can enhance one's knowledge base, inspire innovation, and create opportunities for collaboration that transcend geographical boundaries.

Building and maintaining professional networks requires deliberate strategies, both online and offline. Online networking has gained prominence with the rise of social media and professional networking platforms. LinkedIn, for instance, has become a vital tool for professionals to connect, share content, and engage in industry-specific discussions. To optimize their LinkedIn presence, individuals should ensure their profiles are complete and up to date, highlighting their skills, experiences, and accomplishments. Regularly sharing relevant content, participating in discussions, and endorsing others' skills can increase visibility and credibility within one's professional community.

Offline networking remains equally important. Attending industry conferences, seminars, workshops, and networking events provides opportunities to meet professionals face-to-face, establish rapport, and build relationships based on mutual interests and goals. Volunteering for industry associations, joining professional groups, and participating in local meetups are effective ways to expand one's network. The key is to approach networking with a genuine interest in others, listening actively, and offering help or insights where possible. Building a network is a reciprocal process; the more value one provides, the more likely they are to receive support and opportunities in return.

Personal branding plays a crucial role in career development. In a crowded job market, a strong personal brand differentiates an individual from others, showcasing their unique skills, values, and professional persona. Social media platforms are powerful tools for personal branding. By consistently sharing insightful content, engaging with thought leaders, and participating in industry discussions, individuals can position themselves as experts in their fields. A personal website or blog can further enhance one's brand, providing a platform to showcase their work, share their ideas, and connect with a broader audience.

Creating a compelling online presence involves several practical steps. For students and professionals, developing a personal website or online portfolio is an excellent way to highlight achievements, projects, and skills. Platforms like WordPress, Squarespace, and Wix offer user-friendly tools to create professional websites. Including a blog section allows individuals to share their thoughts on industry trends, providing additional value to their audience and demonstrating thought leadership.

Optimizing LinkedIn profiles is another critical step. This includes using a professional photo, writing a compelling headline and summary, and detailing work experiences and accomplishments. Adding multimedia elements such as videos, presentations, and articles can make a profile more engaging. Recommendations and endorsements from colleagues and mentors add credibility and can positively influence potential employers or collaborators.

As we look toward the future of work, the evolution of social networking platforms will likely continue to shape how professionals connect, collaborate, and build their personal brands. Given the success of platforms like TikTok in capturing the attention and engagement of younger audiences through short-form, dynamic content, it is plausible to imagine a professional social network that leverages similar features. A TikTok-inspired professional social network could indeed work in the future of work, offering unique benefits and addressing some of the limitations of current professional networking platforms.

Such a platform would emphasize short, engaging videos to share professional insights, showcase skills, and connect with others. Professionals could create short videos to share updates about their projects, insights into industry trends, or quick tutorials on specific skills. This format would make it easier for users to consume content on the go and stay updated with the latest developments in their field. The use of short videos would encourage creativity and make content more engaging compared to traditional text-based updates.

Users could upload short clips demonstrating their skills, such as coding a program, designing a graphic, or presenting a business idea. These video portfolios would provide a more dynamic and authentic representation of a professional's capabilities than a static resume. Potential employers or collaborators could easily browse these clips to identify talent and assess their skills in action.

The platform could partner with educational institutions and companies to offer bite-sized learning modules and micro-credentials. Users could watch short instructional videos, complete quick assessments, and earn badges or certificates that are displayed on their profiles. This approach would promote continuous learning and skill development in an accessible format.

Short video introductions and pitches could make networking more personal and effective. Users could create introductory videos to connect with others in their industry, join discussions, or seek mentorship. Collaborative projects could be showcased through video updates, allowing team members to share progress and celebrate milestones.

Just like TikTok, this professional network could have features for real-time engagement, such as likes, comments, shares, and duets. Users could provide instant feedback on each other's content, fostering a community of support and collaboration. This interactive element would make networking more dynamic and engaging.

Leveraging advanced AI algorithms, the platform could recommend relevant content, connections, and opportunities based on user interests, skills, and activity. Personalized content feeds would help users discover valuable resources and connections tailored to their professional goals.

Professionals could use the platform to celebrate their achievements and milestones, such as completing a significant project, receiving a promotion, or earning a certification. These updates could be shared through short, celebratory videos, creating a positive and motivational atmosphere.

To ensure the platform maintains a professional tone, it would implement strict guidelines and moderation policies. Users would be encouraged to share content relevant to their careers and industries, with features designed to maintain a balance between authenticity and professionalism.

Imagine a marketing professional named Daniel who wants to showcase his expertise in digital marketing. On this platform, Daniel uploads a series of short videos demonstrating his skills in social media strategy, content creation, and data analysis. He shares quick tips on optimizing ad campaigns, uses analytics tools to show real-time results, and provides mini tutorials on effective storytelling techniques. His videos gain traction, attracting followers from various companies interested in his expertise.

Meanwhile, Laura, a graphic designer, uses the platform to display her design portfolio through dynamic video presentations. She showcases her design process, from initial sketches to final products, and shares time-lapse videos of her working on creative projects. Potential clients and employers view her videos, impressed by her skills and creativity, leading to freelance opportunities and job offers.

Overall, a TikTok-style professional social network could revolutionize how professionals showcase their skills, connect with others, and stay updated in their fields. By combining the engaging, short-form content format with professional networking features, such a platform would cater to the evolving needs of the modern workforce, fostering a more dynamic, interactive, and visually rich professional environment.

Collaborative Learning and Industry Partnerships

In the rapidly evolving landscape of the future job market, the need for closer collaboration between educational institutions and industries is becoming increasingly critical. Ensuring that students develop relevant skills that align with industry demands requires a proactive approach where academia and business work hand-in-hand. This synergy enhances the educational experience and bridges the gap between theoretical knowledge and practical application, better preparing students for the challenges and opportunities of the modern workforce.

Successful partnerships between universities, companies, and other organizations are already paving the way for this collaborative learning model. For instance, the partnership between MIT and Boeing on the development of cutting-edge aerospace technologies allows students to work on real-world projects, gaining hands-on experience and exposure to industry standards. Similarly, Stanford University's collaboration with Google provides students with opportunities to engage in groundbreaking research in AI, allowing them to benefit from the resources and expertise of one of the world's leading tech companies.

These partnerships bring numerous benefits, including mentorship programs where industry professionals guide students through their educational and career journeys. Mentorships offer invaluable insights into industry practices, helping students build networks and develop the soft skills essential for professional success. Internships and co-op placements further enhance this experience, allowing students to immerse themselves in a professional environment, apply their academic learning in real-world contexts, and gain practical skills that are highly valued by employers.

Industry-sponsored projects are another effective way to integrate practical experience into academic programs. Companies can provide real-world problems for students to solve, fostering a learning environment that emphasizes critical thinking, problem-solving, and innovation. This approach not only enriches the student learning experience but also offers companies fresh perspectives and potential solutions to their challenges. For example, IBM's collaboration with various universities on blockchain technology projects allows students to work on practical applications of emerging technologies, preparing them for future roles in a rapidly growing field.

Alumni networks and professional associations also play a pivotal role in facilitating ongoing learning and career growth. Alumni who have successfully transitioned into the workforce can provide mentorship, career advice, and networking opportunities to current students. They serve as role models and sources of inspiration, demonstrating the practical pathways to career success. Professional associations, on the other hand, offer continuous learning opportunities through workshops, conferences, and certification programs, ensuring that individuals remain current with industry trends and advancements.

Collaborative learning and industry partnerships also contribute to the development of a more adaptive and responsive educational system. By maintaining a close relationship with industry, educational institutions can continuously update their curricula to reflect the latest technological advancements and market needs. This ensures that graduates are equipped with the skills and knowledge required to thrive in their chosen fields. For instance, Northeastern University's emphasis on experiential learning through its co-op program integrates classroom study with professional experience, allowing students to alternate between academic terms and full-time employment in their field of study. This model ensures that students graduate with a robust combination of theoretical knowledge and practical experience, making them highly competitive in the job market.

Moreover, these collaborations foster a culture of innovation and entrepreneurship. By working on real-world projects and engaging with industry professionals, students are encouraged to think creatively and develop innovative solutions. This entrepreneurial mindset is crucial in a world where new challenges and opportunities arise constantly. Programs like the University of California, Berkeley's SkyDeck accelerator provide students and alumni with resources, mentorship, and funding to turn their innovative ideas into successful startups, demonstrating the powerful impact of collaborative learning environments.

Collaborative learning and industry partnerships are essential for preparing students for the future job market. By working closely with industry, educational institutions can ensure that their programs remain relevant, dynamic, and aligned with market needs. Mentorship programs, internships, co-op placements, and industry-sponsored projects provide students with invaluable real-world experience, bridging the gap between academia and the professional world. Alumni networks and professional associations further support ongoing learning and career development. This integrated approach not only enhances the educational experience but also equips students with the skills, knowledge, and networks necessary to thrive in a rapidly changing world.

Will Jobs Exist in 2050?

As we approach the end of this exploration, I want to offer a bold and informed projection on how jobs will evolve from today to 2050, leveraging the knowledge and insights available today. I aim to provide a daring yet thoughtful prediction, breaking down the timeline into five-year increments to map out the anticipated transformations in the job market and workforce dynamics. This journey will encompass the rise of AI, the changing nature of work, and the societal shifts that will accompany these technological advancements.

2025-2030: The Rise of Comprehensive Automation

By 2030, advancements in artificial intelligence and robotics have reached new heights. Companies have begun to adopt fully automated systems that handle manufacturing, logistics, and even complex analytical tasks. The widespread deployment of autonomous vehicles replaces millions of driving jobs globally. Warehouses and factories become almost entirely automated, reducing the need for human labor significantly.

2030-2035: AI Integration into White-Collar Jobs

In the early 2030s, AI systems capable of performing sophisticated tasks in finance, law, and medicine emerge. AI doctors diagnose and treat patients with higher accuracy than their human counterparts. Legal AI systems handle contract reviews, legal research, and even dispute resolution. Financial AI manages investments, banking, and economic forecasting with unprecedented precision. These AI systems are adopted rapidly due to their efficiency and cost-effectiveness, leading to a sharp decline in white-collar jobs.

2035-2040: The Decline of Traditional Employment Models

As AI systems prove their reliability and superiority, businesses start to restructure. The traditional model of full-time employment becomes obsolete. Gig economy platforms evolve, connecting individuals to short-term tasks that AI cannot yet perform. However, the demand for these tasks diminishes as AI continues to improve. Governments and educational institutions struggle to keep up with the pace of change, leaving many workers unprepared for the new economy.

2040-2045: Universal Basic Income Implementation

Facing massive unemployment and social unrest, many countries have begun to implement Universal Basic Income (UBI) policies. UBI provides a safety net for those who have lost their jobs to automation, ensuring everyone has a basic standard of living. This shift allows people to pursue passions, hobbies, and creative endeavors without the pressure of traditional employment. Society begins to value contributions to arts, culture, and community engagement more highly.

2045-2050: The Era of Human Flourishing

By 2045, the concept of a job as we know it has largely disappeared. AI handles the majority of work, from mundane tasks to complex problem-solving. People are no longer defined by their occupations but by their interests and contributions to society. Education systems focus on personal development, creativity, and emotional intelligence. Communities thrive on collaboration and shared goals, fostering a sense of belonging and purpose.

In this new era, human potential is unleashed in unprecedented ways. People have the freedom to explore their passions, engage in lifelong learning, and contribute to their communities in meaningful ways. The economy evolves to support these pursuits, with AI systems ensuring that basic needs are met, and society remains functional and prosperous.

As the disappearance of jobs unfolds, societal responses will vary, encompassing a range of emotions and actions from fear and resistance to adaptation and innovation. Here's a detailed projection of how society might respond and the strategies to overcome the resulting concerns:

Initial Reactions and Resistance (2025-2035)

In the initial stages, as automation begins to replace more jobs, society will likely witness widespread protests and public outcry. Workers from various sectors will voice their concerns over job security and economic stability. Historical parallels can be drawn from the Industrial Revolution and the early 20th century labor movements, where technological advancements led to significant social upheaval. In response to public pressure, governments will take immediate action. Politicians will campaign on promises to protect jobs and may initially impose regulations to slow down the adoption of automation. Legislative measures could include subsidies for industries that retain human workers or taxes on companies that heavily rely on automation. These steps, however, might only provide temporary relief.

Transition Period: From Resistance to Adaptation (2035-2045)

As it becomes clear that automation is inevitable, governments will shift their focus to mitigating its impact. The implementation of Universal Basic Income (UBI) will be a pivotal strategy. UBI will provide financial security to those displaced by automation, ensuring that basic needs are met and reducing the economic strain on affected individuals. Countries like Finland and Canada have already experimented with UBI, suggesting its potential effectiveness on a larger scale.

To facilitate a smoother transition, there will be significant investments in education and reskilling programs. Governments and private sectors will collaborate to create lifelong learning platforms that equip individuals with the skills needed for the new economy. This includes digital literacy, coding, data analysis, and other high-demand skills. Countries with strong education systems, like Finland and Singapore, could serve as models for these initiatives.

Businesses will play a crucial role in this transition. Companies will be encouraged or mandated to invest in their employees' development and reskilling. Corporate social responsibility (CSR) initiatives will expand to include programs aimed at preparing the workforce for the future. Some forward-thinking companies may even pioneer these efforts, gaining public support and enhancing their brand reputation.

Long-Term Adaptation and Flourishing (2045-2050)

As traditional jobs disappear, society will undergo a cultural transformation. The value placed on work will shift from economic necessity to personal fulfillment and community engagement. People will find new purposes in creative endeavors, volunteer work, and lifelong learning. This cultural shift will be supported by educational reforms that emphasize holistic development over mere vocational training.

With the rise of UBI and the reduction of work hours, people will have more time to invest in their communities. Local initiatives, community projects, and cooperative living arrangements will become more common. This will help strengthen social bonds and create support networks that can help individuals navigate the changes brought about by automation.

Governments will adopt new technologies to manage and support this societal transformation. AI and big data analytics will be used to efficiently distribute UBI, manage social services, and predict future educational and employment trends. This will ensure that policies remain responsive to the changing needs of society.

Ensuring an inclusive transition will be crucial. Policymakers will need to address disparities that might arise, ensuring that marginalized groups are not left behind. This includes creating policies that support diverse communities, provide equitable access to resources, and foster an inclusive environment where everyone can thrive.

In the future landscape we've envisioned, the roles of management and leadership within companies will indeed undergo significant transformation, but they are unlikely to disappear entirely. Here's how I foresee the evolution of these roles during the timeframe we've discussed, focusing on the period up to 2050:

2030-2040: AI-Assisted Decision Making

By the early 2030s, AI and advanced analytics will become integral to management roles. Leaders will leverage AI to make more informed decisions, utilizing real-time data analytics, predictive modeling, and machine learning algorithms. These technologies will provide insights into market trends, employee performance, and operational efficiencies, allowing managers to make more strategic decisions with greater accuracy and speed.

AI will also assist in automating routine administrative tasks, such as scheduling, reporting, and performance reviews, freeing managers to focus on more strategic and human-centric aspects of their roles. This augmentation will enhance their capabilities rather than replace them.

2040-2045: Transition to Human-Centric Leadership

As AI handles more of the technical and analytical aspects of management, the role of leaders will shift towards fostering human-centric environments. Emotional intelligence, empathy, and interpersonal skills will become paramount. Leaders will focus on mentoring, team cohesion, and fostering a positive organizational culture. They will act as facilitators, enabling employees to leverage AI tools effectively and ensuring that teams remain motivated and engaged.

The skill set required for leadership will evolve to emphasize creativity, critical thinking, and the ability to inspire and lead diverse, often remote, teams. Leaders will need to be adept at managing virtual teams and creating a sense of community and belonging, even when team members are geographically dispersed.

2045-2050: Leadership in an AI-Driven Economy

In the latter half of this transition, traditional hierarchical structures may give way to more fluid and dynamic organizational models. Leadership roles will be more project-based, with leaders stepping in to guide teams for specific initiatives rather than overseeing continuous operations. This shift will require leaders to be adaptable, continuously updating their skills and approaches to fit the needs of each project and team.

Furthermore, with Universal Basic Income (UBI) and the reduction of traditional work hours, leadership will increasingly involve facilitating purpose-driven projects. Leaders will help align team efforts with broader societal goals, such as sustainability, community development, and innovation. The role of a leader will extend beyond the confines of a single organization, encompassing broader networks and collaborations across various industries and sectors.

A significant aspect of future leadership will involve ensuring the ethical use of AI and fostering inclusivity. Leaders will be responsible for addressing the ethical implications of AI in the workplace, such as bias in decision-making algorithms and the impact on employee privacy. They will need to advocate for transparency and accountability in AI applications, ensuring that technology is used to benefit all stakeholders equitably.

Moreover, leaders will play a crucial role in promoting diversity and inclusion within their organizations. As AI tools become more prevalent, it will be essential to ensure that these technologies do not perpetuate existing biases or inequalities. Leaders will need to champion initiatives that foster diverse perspectives and create an inclusive environment where all employees feel valued and empowered.

Conclusion

As we close this exploration into the future of work, it becomes evident that we are on the brink of unprecedented changes that will fundamentally reshape employment, skills, and the workplace. The integration of AI, the shift from job markets to skill markets, and the emergence of portable benefits are not mere trends but transformative shifts that will redefine how we work, learn, and live.

The journey from traditional job markets to skill markets marks a profound transformation in how we approach work. In the past, companies sought employees to fill predefined roles, often constrained by rigid job descriptions and organizational hierarchies. However, in the future, the focus will shift toward identifying and leveraging specific skills to complete dynamic, project-based tasks. This transition needs a reevaluation of our current education and training systems, emphasizing the need for continuous learning and adaptability. AI will play a crucial role in this transformation, ensuring precise matching of skills to project needs, fostering a more efficient and innovative workforce.

In this future landscape, traditional resumes and job applications will become obsolete. Instead, individuals will maintain dynamic skill profiles, continuously updated with new competencies and experiences. AI-driven platforms will assess and verify these skills, providing an accurate and unbiased representation of a person's abilities. This shift toward a skill-based economy will democratize opportunities, allowing individuals to showcase their talents without the constraints of traditional credentials or geographic limitations. As a result, the job market will become more fluid and meritocratic, where talent and capability are the primary currencies.

Portable benefits will become a cornerstone of the future work environment, addressing the vulnerabilities faced by both full-time employees and freelancers. The establishment of universal benefits accounts will ensure that all workers, regardless of their employment status, have access to essential services such as health insurance, retirement savings, and paid leave. These accounts will be maintained independently of any single employer, with contributions coming from multiple sources. Governments, employers, and workers themselves will collectively contribute to these accounts, creating a robust safety net that follows individuals throughout their careers.

Additionally, worker cooperatives will emerge as powerful entities that negotiate group rates for benefits, leveraging collective bargaining power to secure better terms for their members. These cooperatives will provide a sense of community and mutual support, fostering solidarity among workers from diverse backgrounds. Government-sponsored programs will further enhance this system, offering baseline benefits that ensure no worker is left behind. These initiatives will be supported by international agreements on taxation and funding, ensuring the sustainability and portability of benefits across borders.

The future of education will also undergo a significant overhaul, focusing on developing critical thinking, creativity, and EQ alongside technical skills. The traditional model of education, with its emphasis on rote learning and standardized testing, will give way to more personalized and experiential learning pathways. Online learning platforms, micro-credentials, and flexible learning pathways will enable individuals to acquire new skills and knowledge continuously. Educational institutions will partner with industries to offer real-world learning experiences, bridging the gap between theory and practice.

Project-based learning, internships, and co-op placements will become integral components of educational programs, providing students with hands-on experience and exposure to real-world challenges. These experiences will not only enhance technical proficiency but also foster essential soft skills such as communication, collaboration, and leadership. Interdisciplinary learning will be encouraged, allowing students to draw connections between different fields and develop holistic problem-solving abilities.

Networking and personal branding will play a pivotal role in career development. In a globalized, interconnected job market, the ability to build and maintain professional networks will be crucial. Social media platforms and professional networking sites will enable individuals to connect with peers, mentors, and potential employers across the globe. Personal branding will help individuals differentiate themselves in a competitive market, showcasing their unique skills, values, and professional personas. Building a strong online presence through platforms like LinkedIn, personal websites, and digital portfolios will become essential for career advancement.

Collaborative learning and industry partnerships will further enhance the educational experience. By working closely with industry partners, educational institutions can ensure that their programs remain relevant and aligned with market needs. Mentorship programs, industry-sponsored projects, and alumni networks will provide students with valuable insights, guidance, and connections. These collaborations will foster a culture of innovation and entrepreneurship, encouraging students to think creatively and develop solutions to real-world problems.

The rise of remote work and the global talent pool will redefine the concept of the workplace. Offices will become more flexible and dynamic, with teams forming and dissolving based on project needs. The proliferation of coworking spaces and virtual collaboration tools will enable individuals to work from anywhere, breaking down geographical barriers and fostering a more inclusive and diverse workforce. This shift toward remote and hybrid work models will also have significant ecological benefits, reducing the need for daily commutes and lowering carbon emissions.

As we envision this future, we must also consider the ethical and social implications of these changes. Ensuring fair and equitable access to opportunities, addressing potential disparities in skill distribution, and fostering inclusive growth will be essential. The rise of AI and automation presents both opportunities and challenges, and it is our responsibility to navigate this transition thoughtfully and inclusively. Ethical considerations will guide the development and deployment of AI technologies, ensuring that they are used to augment human capabilities rather than replace them.

The future of work holds immense potential for innovation, creativity, and personal fulfillment. By embracing these changes and proactively preparing for the evolving landscape, we can create a work environment that is not only more efficient and productive but also more humane and fulfilling. The insights and strategies discussed in this book aim to provide a roadmap for navigating this future, ensuring that we are not merely reacting to changes but actively shaping a world of work that benefits everyone.

In the words of Alvin Toffler, "The illiterate of the 21st century will not be those who cannot read and write, but those who cannot learn, unlearn, and relearn." As we stand at the cusp of this new era, let us embrace the opportunities to learn, adapt, and thrive in the inevitable future of work. Together, we can build a future where work is not just a means of survival but a source of inspiration, purpose, and growth.

References

1- Russo, A. (2020, October 20). Recession and automation changes our future of work, but there are jobs coming, report says. World Economic Forum. https://www.weforum.org/press/2020/10/recession-and-automation-changes-our-future-of-work-but-there-are-jobs-coming-report-says-52c5162fce/

2- Illanes, P., Lund, S., Mourshed, M., Rutherford, S., & Tyreman, M. (2018, January 22). Retraining and reskilling workers in the age of automation. McKinsey & Company. https://www.mckinsey.com/featured-insights/future-of-work/retraining-and-reskilling-workers-in-the-age-of-automation

3- Wid.world. (2022). World Inequality Report. https://wir2022.wid.world/

4- Economic Policy Institute. (2022, October). The productivity-pay gap. https://www.epi.org/productivity-pay-gap/#:~:text=From%201979%20to%202020%2C%20net,another%20important%20piece%20of%20information

5- Manyika, J., Lund, S., Chui, M., Bughin, J., Woetzel, L., Batra, P., Ko, R., & Sanghvi, S. (2017, November). Jobs lost, jobs gained: What the future of work will mean for jobs, skills, and wages. McKinsey Global Institute. https://www.mckinsey.com/featured-insights/future-of-work/jobs-lost-jobs-gained-what-the-future-of-work-will-mean-for-jobs-skills-and-wages

6- United Nations. (n.d.). Think Lab on Living Wage. https://unglobalcompact.org/what-is-gc/our-work/livingwages/think-lab-on-living-wage#:~:text=According%20to%20the%20International%20Labour,or%20moderate%20poverty%20in%202019

7- Parmelee, M. (2021, June). The Deloitte Global 2021 Millennial and Gen Z Survey: Highlights. Deloitte Insights. https://www2.deloitte.com/us/en/insights/topics/talent/deloitte-millennial-survey-2021.html

8- Coworking Resources. (2020). Global coworking growth study. https://www.coworkingresources.org/blog/key-figures-coworking-growth

9- Hunt, V., Layton, D., & Prince, S. (2015, January). Why diversity matters. McKinsey & Company. https://www.mckinsey.com/capabilities/people-and-organizational-performance/our-insights/why-diversity-matters

10- Lorenzo, R., Voigt, N., Tsusaka, M., Krentz, M., & Abouzahr, K. (2018, January). How diverse leadership teams boost innovation. Boston Consulting Group. https://www.bcg.com/publications/2018/how-diverse-leadership-teams-boost-innovation

11- Parmelee, M. (2019, May). A generation disrupted. Highlights from the 2019 Deloitte Global Millennial Survey. Deloitte Insights. https://www2.deloitte.com/us/en/insights/topics/talent/deloitte-millennial-survey-2019.html

12-Glassdoor. (2021). 40+ stats for companies to keep in mind for 2021. https://www.glassdoor.com/employers/resources/hr-and-recruiting-stats/#diversity-inclusion-and-belonging

www.ingramcontent.com/pod-product-compliance
Lightning Source LLC
LaVergne TN
LVHW051440050326
832903LV00030BD/3185